"Rabbi Jonathan Kligler's reading into the stories, verses, words, and images of the Torah creates a special work of wonderfully deep personal insights woven with teachings from the wealth of Jewish tradition. Imbued with a spiritual demand to find meaning to Torah in our real lived experience, these teachings do not shun from engaging the readers with difficult and perplexing passages. I find it educating, humorous, and moving."

—Melila Hellner-Eshed
Professor of Jewish Mysticism and Zohar, Hebrew University, Jerusalem; author of *And a River Flows from Eden: On the Language of Mystical Experience in the Zohar*

"Jonathan Kligler has mastered the immersive practice of midrash. He plunges into the ocean of the Torah; he identifies the ancient rivers that fed into its vast extent; he registers awe before the geysers emerging from its depths. To this classic approach, Rabbi Kligler adds a talent for encapsulation, focus, and intelligent summary. Profound and succinct at the same time, *Turn It and Turn It* brings the reader into the confidence of a mature explorer whose originality serves a life-long quest for the fulfilling truth of the Torah."

—Bruce Chilton
Professor of Philosophy and Religion, Bard College; author of *Rabbi Jesus*

"Whether analyzing a biblical text, or a comment of Rashi, or a talmudic meditation on a biblical verse, Rabbi Jonathan Kligler, a superb teacher, makes it clear again, again, and yet again, why Torah study makes a person deeper in every sense: more intellectually accomplished, more empathetic, and, in the final analysis, not just a smarter person, but—and this is what really counts—a finer person."

—Joseph Telushkin
author of *Rebbe* and *Words that Hurt, Words that Heal*

D1519735

"Imagine fifty-four readily accessible steps on the road to a richer spiritual life—each rooted in Scripture and informed by their author's years of deep reading and reflection—and you get this very special book by Rabbi Jonathan Kligler, which not only generously offers its own wise answers, but will inspire you to find your own."

—Brad Hirschfield

President, National Jewish Center for Learning and Leadership; author of *You Don't Have to Be Wrong for Me to Be Right: Finding Faith Without Fanaticism*

"In this lovely and moving exploration of a year's worth of Torah portions, Rabbi Jonathan Kligler weaves together traditional approaches with contemporary insights from both the academic world and his own experience to illustrate the open-ended and transformative possibilities of Torah study."

—Deborah Waxman

President, Reconstructing Judaism

TURN IT
AND
TURN IT

FOR EVERYTHING IS IN IT

TURN IT
AND
TURN IT

FOR EVERYTHING IS IN IT

ESSAYS ON THE WEEKLY
TORAH PORTION

JONATHAN KLIGLER

RECONSTRUCTIONIST
PRESS

WIPF & STOCK · Eugene, Oregon

TURN IT AND TURN IT FOR EVERYTHING IS IN IT
Essays on the Weekly Torah Portion

Wipf & Stock
An Imprint of Wipf and Stock Publishers
199 W. 8th Ave., Suite 3
Eugene, OR 97401

www.wipfandstock.com

PAPERBACK ISBN: 978-1-7252-5107-6
HARDCOVER ISBN: 978-1-7252-5108-3
EBOOK ISBN: 978-1-7252-5109-0

Manufactured in the U.S.A.   FEBRUARY 5, 2020

Dedicated to my mother of blessed memory,
Deborah Kligler Krasnow, 1928–2018.
Mom, when I write, even now I write for you.

Contents

Leviticus

Numbers

Deuteronomy

A Note on God Language

IN THE COURSE OF this book, I utilize many different metaphors and names when referring to God. This is intentional; the very idea that we can accurately and singularly name that which is infinite is absurd. In offering multiple names for God, I follow in the steps of the Torah and later Jewish practice. The Torah's lexicon of God names is rich and poetic (see my commentary on *Parashat Haazinu*, p. 202), and in every age since the Jewish tradition has continued to coin a plethora of new metaphors for the Divine.

The most essential name for God in the Torah is יהוה, known as the Tetragrammaton, or four-letter name. This name has been rendered by Christians into English as Jehovah and by modern scholars as Yahweh, but in the Jewish tradition יהוה is not meant to be pronounced, as it is the ineffable name of God. Therefore, whenever יהוה appears religious Jews substitute אֲדֹנָי *Adonai*. *Adonai* then translates into English as "Lord." *Adonai* and "Lord" have become so ubiquitous that they, too, have become treated as God's name. To me and many others, therefore, these terms have lost their efficacy in evoking the wordless wonder of encountering the Divine. As a remedy, I have chosen to follow the contemporary practice of inserting the English letters YHVH—the English counterparts to יהוה—when referring to Judaism's most sacred name for God. The reader is meant to take pause at each of these encounters as a reminder that the Infinite defies any definition that a typical name might provide. Hopefully, this usage will help forestall any of the glib certainties that fixed language inevitably evokes in us, and keep us alert to the ineffable mystery out of which our lives and this entire cosmos have emerged.

In these pages, I often refer to God as "Life Unfolding." This is my own coinage, based on my understanding of a central teaching of the Torah about the nature of God. In Exodus, Chapter 3, Moses encounters the burning bush and receives his call to free the slaves. Moses directly asks for God's name, and God answers אֶהְיֶה אֲשֶׁר אֶהְיֶה—*Ehyeh Asher Ehyeh*. This is difficult to translate and has been traditionally rendered as "I Am That I Am" or "I Will Be What I Will Be." This is remarkable: God's truest name is not a noun, but a verb! God is not a person or an entity, but rather an action, an energy.

My understanding of the grammar of biblical Hebrew makes for an even richer translation. Biblical Hebrew does not employ past, present and future tenses in the same way as we are accustomed to in English. Rather, it focuses on the perfect and imperfect tenses, meaning actions that have been completed and actions that are still in process. *Ehyeh Asher Ehyeh* is the future imperfect tense, an action that is continuous or ongoing. Therefore, I render *Ehyeh Asher Ehyeh* as "I Am Becoming That Which I Am Becoming."

So, rather than "I Am," which is static, or "I Will Be," which is yet to occur, *Ehyeh Asher Ehyeh* is meant to convey to us that God—the fiery energy that animates the burning bush—is the infinite energy of life that is always coursing, always present, never completed and without limit in time or space. Hence, Life Unfolding. For me, this metaphor evokes the essence of the Divine Name.

A Note on Hebrew Translation

HEBREW IS A WONDERFULLY layered language based on "root" words. Every "root" word comprises a constellation of potential meanings, and the "root" can grow into an entire tree of different but related Hebrew words, each of which, though bearing its own specific usage, also bears the imprint of all the other words of that tree.

There is more: The Torah scroll was originally composed without vowels, a practice that handwritten Torah scrolls still follow today. (Vowels for Hebrew were not invented until the eighth century.) Students of Torah have always engaged in countless creative readings and discussions about the many different ways that certain words and phrases in the Torah might be pronounced, and the various meanings those readings held. Thus, the ancient keepers of the Torah text were already involved in creative readings—and even intentional mis-readings—of the Torah in order to derive new interpretations.

All of which is to say that the Jewish approach to Hebrew is playful. There's a reason why Jews love to play with words; it is a tradition as old as the Torah. The Hebrew letters are considered to be the very building blocks of creation; in Genesis, God speaks Hebrew, and the world comes into being! That is why Judaism refers to Hebrew as *lashon hakodesh*—the "sacred tongue," an endlessly creative template for understanding the world and its secrets.

I take full advantage of this rich heritage in my translations in this volume. I usually begin with the fine translation in *The Torah: A Modern Commentary* (CCAR Press, David E. S. Stein, editor) and then alter the translations as seem most accurate to me. I allow myself to use creative translations where I see fit to strengthen the particular reading that I am emphasizing in that particular teaching. I celebrate the multiple and authentic ways in which the Hebrew can be understood. I encourage readers to look at multiple translations of the Torah (there are many) to get a feeling for the variety of lenses through which Torah can be translated and understood.

Acknowledgements

THANK YOU TO KENNETH Wapner for his skillful and thoughtful editing of this volume, and for his many years of encouragement to me to pursue my writing.

Thank you to Karen Levine for her always thoughtful advice and skillful work in moving this project forward. Karen is a wonderful collaborator, and I could not have accomplished this without her.

Thank you as well to Elena Erber of Thinking Partners for designing the cover and creating the website that accompanies this volume. Elena has been a treasured collaborator on all of my creative projects for many years.

Thank you to the board of directors of Kehillat Lev Shalem, the Woodstock Jewish Congregation, where I have served for 30 years, for giving their complete support to my writing and scholarship endeavors. And thank you to all of my dedicated Torah students at the congregation; most of the ideas in this volume were developed in the animated back-and-forth exchanges of our Torah-study classes and discussions.

Thank you to my wife, Ellen Jahoda, for putting her discerning eye and ear to many of the essays in this collection, always able to pick up a false note and point it out to me. I also am thrilled that Ellen's artful papercuts grace this volume. And thank you to our beloved daughters, Timna and Nomi, now both launched, for being their wonderful selves. Extra thanks to Nomi for her skillful assistance with design.

Thank you to my parents, Herb and the late Deborah Krasnow, whose financial support makes this publication possible, and who have always believed in me, advised me wisely and cheered me on.

Thank you to all of my teachers and to my many colleagues, especially from Reconstructing Judaism and from the Institute for Jewish Spirituality, who have turned and turned the Torah with me, revealing countless fresh insights prompted by their passion, intelligence, and open minds and hearts.

Thank you to the Reconstructionist Press for publishing this book. The philosophy of Reconstructionism has guided and fully informed my rabbinate, and I feel strongly that *Turn It and Turn It* has found its appropriate home in the Reconstructionist Press catalogue. You can learn more about Reconstructionist Judaism at: reconstructingjudaism.org.

Introduction

בֶּן בַּג בַּג אוֹמֵר, הֲפָךְ בָּה וַהֲפָךְ בָּה, דְּכֹלָּא בָה. וּבָהּ תֶּחֱזֵי,
וְסִיב וּבְלֵה בָהּ, וּמִנַּהּ לֹא תָזוּעַ, שֶׁאֵין לְךָ מִדָּה טוֹבָה הֵימֶנָּה:

*Ben Bag Bag omeir: hafokh bah v'hafokh bah, d'khola
vah; u'vah tekhezei, v'siv u'vleih vah, u'minah lo tazua,
she'ein lekha midah tovah heimenah.*

Ben Bag Bag taught: Turn it and turn it, for everything is in it;
reflect on it, grow old and gray in it, do not depart from it, for
there is no better path than this (Pirkei Avot, 5:24).

THESE ARE OUR ANCIENT instructions for how to engage with the
Torah. The curiously named Ben Bag Bag's epigram appears at the very
end of the seminal collection of rabbinic wisdom sayings known as *Pirkei
Avot, The Teachings of the Sages.* In concluding the collection with Ben Bag
Bag's words, our sages give his teaching a place of honor. His words serve
as a summation for the entire Jewish enterprise of studying the Torah as a
guidebook for life.

I have followed Ben Bag Bag's dictum. For decades, I have immersed
myself in the Torah, wrestled with the Torah's ambiguous and sometimes
disturbing passages, reveled in the Torah's unfolding and myriad meanings, and am indeed growing older and grayer in my pursuit. The Torah

has become a doorway into passionate conversations spanning thousands of years; a portal into the deepest insights on the human soul; a gateway onto the path of living a righteous and meaningful life; a window into the mystery of consciousness and the nature of the cosmos itself.

In this volume, I share with you some of the fruits of my explorations. I have titled this collection "Turn It and Turn It," and it is my hope that readers will get a sense of the vast range of ways to look at and benefit from studying Torah—from the historical to the mystical, from the political to the deeply personal, from the practical to the poetic.

I inherit an ancient set of methods that form the rabbinic approach, such as wordplay, intense and close readings of the text, and imaginative expansions on the story, known as *midrash*. To this toolkit I add many contemporary approaches and fields of study, including literary criticism, comparative mythology, archaeological discoveries, poetics, anthropology, psychoanalytic theory, even quantum physics. I rely on both ancient and contemporary teachers of Torah to guide me. I study Torah with Christian friends, for whom the Torah is also a foundational text, eager to find out where we differ, and where we actually align in our understanding and our interpretation of the text. I celebrate the multivocal philosophy of the ancient Jewish sages who, when confronted with competing interpretations, claimed a heavenly voice that announced, "Both these and those are the words of the Living God" (Babylonian Talmud, Tractate Eruvin 13b).

In Jewish practice, the Torah is divided into weekly portions, such that in the course of a full year we make our way through the entire Five Books of Moses. In Hebrew, we refer to the weekly portion as the *parshah* or *parashah*, the plural being *parashiyot*. We begin in the beginning every fall at the conclusion of the Jewish Holy Days, and every week we progress until, as a year passes, we reach the end of Deuteronomy. And we begin again. We even have an especially joyous holiday, Simchat Torah, to mark the completion and renewal of the annual cycle of readings. The essays in this volume follow that cycle, with one essay for each parashah, and can be a companion to those of you who wish to follow the annual Jewish rhythm for studying the Torah. Of course, you are completely welcome to read these entries at any pace and in any order you wish.

As a product of the 21st century, this volume is augmented by an active website (rabbijonathankligler.com). On this site, you will be able to access an ever-growing archive of my Torah commentaries, listen to an audio version of this book, and access the many Torah classes that I have taught and recorded in recent years. I hope that the website will serve as an ever-expanding resource for those interested in studying Torah.

There is a Hebrew phrase, שַׁרְשֶׁרֶת הַדֹּורֹות *sharsheret ha'dorot*, the chain of generations. It refers to the ongoing transmission of Torah from the seminal moment at Mount Sinai—not an historical, geographical moment, but rather the birth of our tradition—down through every generation to the present. It is an honor to be able to forge a link in this living tradition.

—RABBI JONATHAN KLIGLER

הרב יהונתן משה בן דוד ודבורה

HaRav Yehonatan Moshe ben David v'Dvorah

Woodstock, N.Y.

בראשית
Genesis

בראשית ברא אלהים את השמים ואת הארץ

In the beginning God created the heavens and the earth.
(Genesis 1:1)

1 ――――――――――――――――――――

Bereishit | בראשית

Behold, It Is Very Good

וַיַּרְא אֱלֹהִים אֶת־כָּל־אֲשֶׁר עָשָׂה וְהִנֵּה־טוֹב מְאֹד

Va'yar Elohim et kol asher asah v'hinei tov me'od

And God looked at all that God had made and behold, it was
very good (Genesis 1:31).

THE TORAH BEGINS, AND the curtain rises on creation. The first chapter
of Genesis is the magnificent overture to the great drama of human life
and striving that will ensue. The language is stately and musical; it should
be read aloud. Beginning in darkness, creation unfolds in ever-expanding
complexity and glory.

God the Creator shapes and conducts creation in seven movements,
which God names "days." And every day, God surveys God's handiwork
and reflects upon it. And the verdict is a ringing affirmation: It is good.

The world is good.

This view of creation will suffuse the entire Torah and will forever be
the foundation of the Jewish worldview. Our world is not something to be
transcended or shunned. It is not merely the anteroom to some truly good
and perfected realm. It is not a meaningless playground for the gods, we

their hapless playthings. No, God has created an orderly universe, and created us and placed us here with moral purpose. This world is our home, and it is good that we are here. This remains true despite our glaring failures, and our deluded and destructive ways. The essential goodness of life abides.

How do we come to recognize this goodness? The key to our understanding is encoded into Genesis's opening. Seven is the organizing principle of the Torah. The careful student of the Torah will find that sets of seven abound, and that this is not accidental. Seven represents completeness and wholeness. The first verse of the Torah, בְּרֵאשִׁית בָּרָא אֱלֹהִים אֵת הַשָּׁמַיִם וְאֵת הָאָרֶץ *Bereishit bara Elohim et hashamayim v'et ha'aretz*—"In the beginning God created the heavens and the earth"—comprises seven Hebrew words; the pattern is set from the first, a seed planted from which the entire Torah will grow. And seven times in the course of the chapter, God surveys creation and sees that it is טוֹב *tov*—good. The chapter ends with this crowning verse:

וַיַּרְא אֱלֹהִים אֶת־כָּל־אֲשֶׁר עָשָׂה וְהִנֵּה־טוֹב מְאֹד וַיְהִי־עֶרֶב וַיְהִי־בֹקֶר יוֹם הַשִּׁשִּׁי:

> *Va'yar Elohim et kol asher asah v'hinei tov me'od. Vay'hi erev vay'hi boker yom hashishi*—"And God looked at all that God had made and behold it was very good! And there was evening and there was morning, the sixth day" (Genesis 1:31).

God makes the world in six days, but creation is not complete without a seventh: a day to contemplate, a day to appreciate, a day to cease from labor and be restored. The Sabbath completes creation. "God blessed the seventh day and made it holy, for on that day God rested from all the work that had been done" (Genesis 2:3). If we work without pausing, if we do not sanctify and dignify our lives with time to reflect, our lives and our humanity are incomplete.

Human beings are God's culminating creation, the final act of the sixth day: "God created the human being in the Divine image, male and female God created them" (Genesis 1:27). God then blesses us and tells us to "be fruitful and multiply, and to fill the earth and domesticate it" (Genesis 1:28). God gives us dominion over the animals and the plants for our benefit and sustenance. One can infer from these instructions that this is what it means to be made in God's image; far beyond any other species, we have been given the capability to shape and control creation. Many have taken these instructions as license as our right and our destiny to exploit the world's resources for our own self-interest. Many blame the Bible for the hubris it engenders in people, as we sully and desecrate the earth as though we have been Divinely empowered to do so.

And if our creation story ended with the sixth day, these interpretations might be valid. But it is the seventh day, Shabbat, that completes and crowns God's creation. To be made in God's image does not only mean that we have been endowed with the power to reshape the world. To be made in God's image also means that we have been endowed with self-awareness, and the capacity to step back and reflect on our actions. And therefore, made as we are in God's image, we, too, must incorporate the consciousness of Shabbat into our lives. If we ignore this commandment, we fail to actualize the Divine image implanted within us. Instead, if we extract and consume the earth's resources without pause, we make a mockery of that Divine image. We lose touch with the goodness that inheres in this world. We worship the works of our own hands, and become petty and false gods. We face the results of that failure today, as our planet convulses under the unending onslaught of our domination.

Shabbat is so essential to the worldview of the Torah that it is included among the Ten Commandments. Not only are we commanded not to work on Shabbat, but we are forbidden to make anyone who serves under us labor. Even beasts of burden must be given a day of rest. We relinquish our control and our will to dominate. We pause and step back to regain our perspective. We stop to smell the roses. We restore our sanity and our souls. Shabbat, the seventh day, completes us, just as it completes creation.

This awareness that we nurture on Shabbat is meant to infuse our consciousness at all times so that while we labor, we do not lose ourselves in the frantic striving, nor mistake our busyness for the full and glorious experience of being alive. For this is a good world, and it is good that we are here.

2 —————————

No'akh | נח

Is There a Measure for Righteousness?

אֵלֶּה תּוֹלְדֹת נֹחַ נֹחַ אִישׁ צַדִּיק תָּמִים הָיָה בְּדֹרֹתָיו אֶת־
הָאֱלֹהִים הִתְהַלֶּךְ־נֹחַ:

Eileh toldot No'akh: No'akh ish tzadik tamim hayah b'dorotav; et ha'Elohim hithalekh No'akh.

These are the generations of Noah: Noah was a righteous man, wholehearted in his generation; Noah walked with God (Genesis 6:9).

THE TORAH PORTION *NO'AKH* (Noah) begins with Genesis Chapter 6, Verse 9. Before exploring some of the interpretations of that verse, let's first ask a more fundamental question: Why would the portion of *No'akh* start in the middle of a chapter?

The answer is that the traditional Jewish division of the Torah into weekly portions long predates the assignment of numbered chapters and verses. Chapters and verses are a medieval and early modern Christian invention. Jewish versions of the Bible adopted this practice during these recent centuries. This numbering practice has no relation to the much older divisions of the Jewish scribal tradition.

Our ancient sages carefully and ingeniously chose the beginning of each week's portion by selecting a verse or section that they found particularly resonant with meaning, often presaging the main themes of that portion. The weekly *parashah* (portion) then derives its name from the first significant word of that first verse—in this week's case, *No'akh*. Traditional commentators make a point of plumbing the very beginning of the *parashah* with the understanding that, even if its deeper meanings are not immediately clear, its selection was in no way arbitrary. We will follow this ancient tradition:

"These are the generations of Noah: Noah was a righteous man, wholehearted in his generation; Noah walked with God" (Genesis 6:9).

Rabbi Shlomo Yitzkhaki, known by the acronym Rashi, lived in northern France during the 11th century and composed the most widely studied of all Torah commentaries. Rashi asks about this verse: "Why does the Torah say that Noah was a righteous man (צַדִּיק *tzaddik*) in his generation? If he was a *tzaddik*, would he not be so no matter what generation he was born into? Why did it not simply say 'Noah was a righteous, wholehearted man?'" Assuming, as Jewish interpretation does, that no phrase or word in the Torah is superfluous, Rashi wants to explain the reason for the use of "in his generation." As always, his explanation is grounded in a sophisticated and intensely close reading of not only this verse, but of the entire Torah. And, as always, Rashi (and the Jewish tradition) assumes that there is more than one answer; that, in fact, the Torah by its sublime nature must contain multiple meanings.

Rashi answers (my paraphrase): Some of our sages interpret "in his generation" favorably. That is, Noah managed to be righteous despite the evil that surrounded him. Had Noah been born in a more righteous generation with more positive influences, he might have become even more righteous! Other sages interpret "in his generation" derogatorily. That is, had Noah been born in Abraham's generation, compared to Abraham, Noah would not have measured up.

There are streams of ancient Jewish thought supporting both of these views, and Rashi cites them both. However, Rashi appears to prefer the derogatory view of Noah and finds his support in the latter part of the same verse, "Noah walked with God." In its plain meaning, this is obviously complimentary of Noah. But Rashi searches the Torah for other places where it describes a character as *hit'halekh*—that is, walking with God. Rashi finds that the same wording is used to describe Abraham's relationship with God, but with a crucial difference:

> But concerning Abraham, Scripture says: Abraham walked before (as in, ahead of) God. Noah walked with God; that is, Noah required God's support to uphold him in righteousness, but Abraham strengthened himself and walked in his righteousness by himself (Rashi on Genesis 6:9).

Abraham's righteousness was self-generated, whereas Noah's depended on God's support. And what, according to this reading, proves this hypothesis? When God instructs Noah to build an ark, God tells Noah that God is going to bring a flood and destroy all that lives on earth, for humans have sullied God's magnificent creation through their immorality and selfishness. In response, Noah follows all of God's instructions but is silent. In contrast, when God tells Abraham about Sodom and Gomorrah's reprehensible immorality, and that God is considering destroying the cities, Abraham is not silent. Abraham approaches God and chastises God!

> Will you indeed sweep away the innocent along with the wicked? What if there are 50 innocent people down there? Will you not spare the city for the sake of the innocent in its midst? Far be it from You to do such a thing, killing innocent and wicked alike. Far be it from you! Must not the judge of all the earth act justly? (Genesis 18:23-25).

What audacity! Abraham gets in God's face and demands that God live up to God's own potential as loving and just. I think we call that *chutzpah*.

In contrast, Noah is silent, compliant to God's commands, but with no apparent ability to stand up independently for all of the innocents who will suffer as a result of God's decree. Hence, the argument that Noah's righteousness is relative to the wicked generation in which he lived.

By this reading, we understand why our tradition considers Abraham our spiritual father and not Noah. Abraham was willing to be in active relationship with God. In the lineage of the Torah, Abraham is the first human willing to question and dispute the so-called Divine Will; Abraham courageously carries a sense of justice in the face of the unfairness of the universe. In the narrative of our Torah, he is the one that God has been waiting for; just as God discerned in the Garden of Eden that the lonely Adam longed for a true intimate partner, so God has been longing for human beings who could be God's intimate partner—God's lover, as it were. In the book of

Isaiah (41:8), God actually refers to Abraham as "my beloved." Abraham is on intimate terms with God. Abraham both adores God and argues with God; Abraham has faith in God and also questions God's judgment. Isn't this what we long for: a true partner in life? Perhaps that is why God says about Abraham, "and you shall be a blessing" (Genesis 12:3).

Abraham is the prototype of יִשְׂרָאֵל *Yisrael*, Israel, which means "God-wrestler," a name we carry even today. But Noah merely obeys, and the innocent perish.

One might say that Noah has a deficit in empathy. "Empathy deficit disorder"—the human capacity to be numb to the suffering of others—might, in fact, be the very source of the evil that God feels compelled to wash away with the Flood. Some commentators somewhat fancifully interpret Noah's sojourn on the ark as God's "treatment plan" for Noah's empathy deficit disorder. Noah is locked up in the ark for a year with the task of feeding and caring for all the animals. In the process, Noah is forced to develop empathy for the needs of all living creatures. Only then is he permitted to leave the ark, for only then is Noah fit to become the new Adam, the new progenitor of the human race.

3 ———————

Lekh-Lekha | לֶךְ־לְךָ

Go to Yourself: Abraham and the Spiritual Journey

וַיֹּאמֶר יְהֹוָה אֶל־אַבְרָם לֶךְ־לְךָ מֵאַרְצְךָ וּמִמּוֹלַדְתְּךָ וּמִבֵּית
אָבִיךָ אֶל־הָאָרֶץ אֲשֶׁר אַרְאֶךָּ:

*Va'yomer YHVH el Avram lekh-lekha me'artzekha
u'mimoladetkha u'mibeit avikha el ha'aretz asher
ar'ekha.*

And YHVH said to Abram, "*Lekh-lekha* (go forth, but literally go to yourself) from your land and from your birthplace
and from your father's house, to the land that I will show you"
(Genesis 12:1).

FOR ME, THE TORAH reveals its deepest lessons when I read it as a spiritual guide rather than a literal history. Whatever historical lessons we learn
from studying Torah are secondary in importance; the lives of its protago-
nists are meant to inform our lives here in the present. The word "Torah"
does not translate as "history" or even "law," but "teaching" or "guidance."

This week's Torah portion begins with God's dramatic call to Abram to go on a life journey that will change him forever. But this potential transformation comes with a price: to pursue this quest, Abram and his wife, Sarai, must leave behind their home, the habitual and head into the unknown.

All of this is intimated in the layered phrase that gives this week's Torah portion its name: לֶךְ-לְךָ *Lekh-Lekha*. לֵךְ *Lekh* means "go." לְךָ *Lekha* means "to you" or "for you." This phrase is difficult to translate, but we might render it colloquially as, "Get thee out!" or "Get yourself going!" However, *lekh-lekha* literally means "go to yourself." The journey of Abraham and Sarah is a spiritual journey, an inward quest for a new way of seeing the world, a journey of perception. As our spiritual father and mother, Abraham and Sarah bequeath to us a sublime idea: that all of reality is informed by a unifying Presence, and that Presence is calling us to greater purpose and awareness. Deeply aware of the ineffability of that Presence, our tradition names it YHVH, Being Itself, or Life Unfolding. Each and every one of us is a unique expression of Life Unfolding, a Child of God, we might say. Judaism insists that we must become aware of this truth in order to fulfill our potential and purpose.

We are finite beings who sense the presence of the Infinite moving within us and all around us. That awareness calls us to fulfill our potential as expressions of infinite life. This calling turns out to be extremely difficult and elusive, and requires of us courage, tenacity, humility and faith. In the Jewish tradition, Abraham is our spiritual father because he perceives this truth, heeds the call and embarks on the journey.

The Torah lets us know that something is stymied or incomplete for Abram and Sarai. For one, their names are incomplete, as though something is missing from their lives. They will only become their full selves, Abraham and Sarah, after many trials. We also learn that they are childless, barren. Abram and Sarai long to be generative, but something remains closed within them. For their barrenness to transform into generativity, they will need to open themselves to Life Unfolding in ways they have not yet discovered.

After many challenges, that opening presents itself at the end of *Lekh-Lekha*. YHVH places the letter ה *hei* into each of their names: Abram becomes Abraham, Sarai becomes Sarah. The Hebrew letter ה is the sound of openness (as in הַלְלוּיָה *halleluyah*), the sound of breath and a key letter in יהוה YHVH, the name of God. Inserted into their very names, Abraham and Sarah, ה *hei* represents an expansion of awareness, the awareness of the presence of God within them as well as all around them.

Along with this expansion, Abraham must also open himself further: He is commanded to circumcise himself. Circumcision, in the Torah, is an act of opening. Moses is said to be of "uncircumcised lips," meaning impeded speech. In an important passage in Deuteronomy, Moses instructs us that we must circumcise our hearts—that is, remove the sheath from around our hearts and stiffen our necks no more, so that we might uphold the cause of the powerless and befriend the stranger. Abraham's circumcision must be understood in this consistent biblical context. It is the sign of his radical willingness to be generously open and deeply committed to Life, to the presence of God in everyone and everything. It is the mark of the covenant that Abraham now willingly enters with YHVH, Life Unfolding. As Abraham's spiritual journey continues, this commitment he now makes to be vulnerable and open is going to allow him and Sarah to conceive a child, to be vessels of life. Yes, the Torah tells us that Abraham is 100 years old, and Sarah is 90. But it is never too late to grow in awareness and love.

Abraham and Sarah heeded the call *lekh-lekha* and embarked on the inward journey towards self-awareness. Every one of us can take that spiritual journey. If we are willing to leave behind limited and habitual conceptions of ourselves, we will discover that we indeed are expressions of infinite life, which animates us and flows through us, the breath of life that is the sound of the letter ה *hei*. We each have a unique and irreplaceable contribution to make, each of us an emanation of Life Unfolding.

4 ⸻

Vayera | וירא

Holding What We Love With Open Arms

וְהָאֱלֹהִים נִסָּה אֶת־אַבְרָהָם וַיֹּאמֶר אֵלָיו אַבְרָהָם וַיֹּאמֶר הִנֵּנִי:
וַיֹּאמֶר קַח־נָא אֶת־בִּנְךָ אֶת־יְחִידְךָ אֲשֶׁר־אָהַבְתָּ אֶת־יִצְחָק
וְלֶךְ־לְךָ אֶל־אֶרֶץ הַמֹּרִיָּה וְהַעֲלֵהוּ שָׁם לְעֹלָה עַל אַחַד הֶהָרִים
אֲשֶׁר אֹמַר אֵלֶיךָ:

*V'ha'Elohim nisah et Avraham va'yomer eilav Avra-
ham, va'yomer hineni. Va'yomer kakh na et binkha
et y'khidkha asher ahavta et Yitzkhak v'lekh lekha
el eretz hamoriah v'ha'aleihu sham l'olah al akhad
heharim asher omar eilekha.*

And God tested Abraham. God said to him, "Abraham," and
Abraham answered, "Here I am." And God said, "Take your
son, your only one, the one you love, Isaac and offer him to me
on a mountain that I will show you" (Genesis 22:1–2).

THE TORAH SPEAKS ON many levels. It is a book of ethics, laws, our
people's ancient history and lore. It is also a book of spiritual wisdom and
guidance. I grew up studying Torah as ethics and laws, and as ancient

history and lore, but only as an adult did I begin to encounter Torah as a wellspring of spiritual wisdom. Our sages compare Torah to a magnificent gemstone with innumerable facets. Every way you turn the gem reveals a new refraction of the meaning of the words, a new glimmering. The longer I study Torah, the more I come to know that this is true: I turn it and turn it like a beautiful gem, the light shines on it and through it, and deeper and deeper insights reveal themselves. Paradoxically, the deeper the insights, the more evanescent they are, the more they slip through my fingers, and the harder they are to put into words. Yet their truth rings in my soul like a bell.

I hope to be studying Torah the rest of my life.

To be available to this realm of Torah, I have had to learn humility, or at least, the beginnings of humility. I was raised and educated to be intellectually arrogant, and to assume that the writings of tribal ancestors must be inherently lacking in sophistication and depth. Still, a question nagged at me: Why would some ancient collection of law and lore still be considered so important unless it contained within it timeless wisdom? Maybe the shortcomings and shortsightedness were at least partly my own. With this admission, I could begin.

That does not mean I then gave up my critical thinking; that would be the opposite of what our tradition requires for Torah study. There is a reason Jews prize thinking! It is central to the Jewish spiritual quest. Not my intellectual acumen, but my intellectual arrogance had to go. That arrogance, which constantly rears its head, must be subdued and replaced by curiosity, wonder and awe.

Let us, then, approach the story of Abraham and his near-sacrifice of his son, Isaac (יִצְחָק Yitzkhak). This story makes most of us shudder, to say the least. Why does our tradition present this story of the Father of our People trying to kill his son? It is so disturbing. And why did our sages require us to read it not only when it arrives in the weekly cycle, but also single it out to be read again on Rosh Hashanah?

In our discomfort, we distance ourselves from the text, try to explain it away, neutralize it, justify it, ignore it . . . but what if the story of Abraham and his son was meant to make us feel uncomfortable? What if the teaching encoded in this story is difficult and uncomfortable? What if the Torah meant to make us squirm? What if some spiritual truths are difficult to confront?

Spiritual teachings of all traditions force us to confront life. We want to be comfortable, to be told that everything is all right; the child in us wants to be reassured. But what if life is inherently a struggle and everything is not all right, and our measure as human beings is taken by how we respond to life's challenges? Perhaps this is the deep wisdom we seek: How are we to respond to life's fundamental and terrible uncertainty? Let us embrace our discomfort and plumb our Torah for guidance.

To read the Torah on this level, we've got to stop being so literal. We must read the story as myth or as dream, full of symbolism and allusions, images pregnant with meaning. We must know that the story is about us. This is what makes it timeless and present. And so, we read: "And God tested Abraham. God said to him, 'Abraham,' and Abraham answered, 'Here I am.' And God said, 'Take your son, your only one, the one you love, Isaac, and offer him up to me on a mountain that I will show you' " (Genesis 22:1–2).

In a conventional reading of the Torah, God is a character in the story—a willful, sometimes benevolent, sometimes harsh parent or potentate who is guiding his creation. But what if we read the passage like this: And Life tested Abraham (or you, or me). Life said to him, "Abraham," and Abraham answered, "Here I am." And Life said, "Take that which is absolutely the most precious to you and be willing to let it go."

To symbolize this test, the Torah chooses the most emotionally loaded figure we can imagine: one's child. And the Torah increases the stakes. Abraham didn't have this child that had been promised him until he was 100 years old, and all the promises of the future are contained in Isaac's being. Take your son, that in which you have invested your deepest attachment, your hopes for the future, your unfinished business, your promise of immortality . . . and be willing to let it go.

Life tests us every day in the most mundane ways. I make a plan for my day. It's a good plan. I'm attached to my plan. The day proceeds, life happens, my kid gets sick and has to be picked up at school, and my plan is soon in complete tatters. I then have two basic options. I can spend the rest of the day frustrated and angry, or I can say: Life, here I am. I offer up to you my hopes and expectations for this day, so that I might be present to the life that has been given to me this moment.

Some days, I rise to the test. Other days, I act like a jerk, petulant and resentful about my good plan being ruined. I'm no fun to be with, and I miss another opportunity to serve Life Unfolding with joy.

Then there are the more difficult tests, not the everyday variety, but the tragedies in our lives: the deaths of loved ones; the losses of illness and disability; house fires, bankruptcies, broken dreams; the deep despair of watching human folly and destruction, and having such limited abilities to help ease human suffering and make the world a better place. And Life tested Abraham: Are you willing to say "Here I am" to these tests, and still serve Life with reverence and joy?

I spoke with my mom of blessed memory about this, and she talked with me about getting older. The trajectory was clear. She was facing, inexorably, one loss after another—the loss of physical abilities, the loss of friends, perhaps the loss of mental acuity, until the ultimate loss, the loss of life.

I don't mean to sound depressing; it's just true. Yet how we have lived each day prepares us for the great tests we face as we age. Life is a harsh taskmaster, and there is no guarantee that we will pass these tests. We all know people who have been trodden under, or embittered or broken or who seem to have given up. As I said, true spiritual teachings do not dance around reality and make nice. The purpose of a religious life is to prepare us to meet our lives and say, "Here I am, what have you got next for me?"

This is Abraham's greatness and the reason we (along with billions of other humans on the planet) consider him our spiritual father: because he was able to respond to Life as it tested him and say הִנֵּנִי *hineni*, "Here I am."

He was not quiescent in his acceptance of Life. Remember, Abraham is renowned for arguing with God over the fate of innocents in Sodom and Gomorrah. Abraham fights faithfully for justice and goodness. Yet Abraham also was willing to accept Life. As with all spiritual teachings, herein lies a crucial paradox: We must love life and all that is in it passionately, and at the same time be willing to let it go. In 1950, as Rabbi Milton Steinberg, of blessed memory, approached an untimely death due to heart disease, he titled his final sermon "To Hold With Open Arms." He instructed his congregation "to hold life at once infinitely precious and yet as a thing to be lightly surrendered ... to clasp the world, but with relaxed hands; to embrace it, but with open arms."

And so, Abraham walks hand in hand with his son, and when his son says, "Father," Abraham responds: "Here I am, my son." Can we hold what we love with open arms, knowing that we might at any time have to release our grip? Perhaps real love is precisely this paradoxical ability to hold with open arms.

In our story, thank God, Abraham does not have to relinquish his son, his hopes, his dreams. The knife is lowered. The cancer goes into remission. The airbags deploy, and no one is killed. But the message is unavoidable: As long as we are alive, loss is unavoidable. May we have the courage to accept this truth, and still open our arms to life and to love.

5 ———————————————

Hayei Sarah | חיי שרה

Equanimity in the Face of Uncertainty

וַיִּהְיוּ חַיֵּי שָׂרָה מֵאָה שָׁנָה וְעֶשְׂרִים שָׁנָה וְשֶׁבַע שָׁנִים שְׁנֵי חַיֵּי
שָׂרָה:

*Va'yihyu hayei Sarah mei'ah shanah v'esrim shanah
v'sheva shanim shnei hayei Sarah.*

And the life of Sarah was one hundred years and twenty
years and seven years; these were the years of the life of Sarah
(Genesis 23:1).

OUR PORTION THIS WEEK is named *Hayei Sarah*, the "Life of Sarah,"
drawn as always from the very first words of the portion. There is an irony
in this title that has fascinated Torah commentators throughout the ages. It
also fascinates me. The portion is about Sarah's death and its aftermath, not
her life. Abraham proceeds to mourn Sarah and purchase a burial site. He
then sends his servant Eliezer to find a wife for Sarah and Abraham's son,
Isaac, and when Eliezer returns with Rebecca, Isaac loves Rebecca and finds
comfort with her after the loss of his mother. Abraham remarries and raises
more children before he passes away at a ripe old age. His sons Isaac and

Ishmael come together to bury their father. Life goes on after Sarah's death, as it should. There is grieving and renewal, loss and continuity.

But the name of our *parashah*—"The Life of Sarah"—prompts us to pause and assess Sarah's life before the inevitable moving on. I would like to examine two prominent streams of interpretation of the text.

Our sages notice that the announcement of Sarah's passing comes immediately after the story of Abraham's binding of Isaac on the altar, and many *midrashim* link the two episodes and conclude that Sarah's death was somehow connected to the near-death of her son. One *midrashic* account tells us,

> So Abraham took Isaac, his son, and led him up hill and down dale, and up to the top of one mountain, and he built an altar and arranged the wood, and took the knife to slaughter him. And had the angel not called out from heaven, Isaac would have been slaughtered! When Isaac returned to his mother Sarah, she asked him where he had been. He told her the entire story. Sarah became unhinged with terror and said, "Are you telling me that had it not been for the angel, you would be dead?" And Isaac said, "Yes." At that, Sarah screamed like the wailing sounds of the shofar, her soul flew away and she died.[1]

This is a shocking reading—Sarah dies because she cannot bear the thought that only a hair's breadth separated her son from death. And yet, this is our reality: Each of us lives a life suspended in uncertainty. Each time our child or our spouse or even our beloved dog ranges out of our sight, we have absolutely no guarantee that they will return intact. How do we continue living?

Avivah Zornberg, in her seminal work *Genesis: The Beginning of Desire,* brilliantly explores this question.[2] Zornberg employs the author Milan Kundera's phrase and explains that Sarah succumbs to "the unbearable lightness of being." The radical uncertainty of our existence is always with us. We work throughout our lives to develop the paradoxical qualities of strength and of acceptance so that we can rise to meet every day. As I described in *Parashat Vayera*, life is always testing us. The "Abraham" in each of us rises with alacrity and acceptance to the daily call to *lekh-lekha*, to go forth into the unknown, while the "Sarah" in each of us just can't take it

---

1. Midrash *Vayikrah Rabbah* 20:2, my free rendering.
2. Avivah Gottlieb Zornberg, *Genesis: The Beginning of Desire*, p. 126-128.

anymore and wants to give up the ghost, *genug shoyn!*—enough already! In this reading, I truly feel for Sarah, and I think I understand.

Another more mystical *midrashic* vein sees Sarah and Abraham not as flawed humans, but as archetypal ideals. This approach addresses the unusual wording that describes Sarah's life: "And the life of Sarah was one hundred years and twenty years and seven years; these were the years of the life of Sarah." Why not just say "one hundred twenty-seven years"? And why is "life" repeated twice? This phrasing is repeated in describing Abraham's passing two chapters later: "These are the days of the years of Abraham's life, that he lived: one hundred years and seventy years and five years. And Abraham breathed his last and died at a ripe old age, fulfilled and at peace" (Gen. 25:7-8).

Abraham and Sarah lived every day of every year. They lived! Together, they represent the ideal of living with faith and trust, of heeding the call of each day to live fully in spite of our lack of control or guarantees. The Hasidic master Rabbi Yehuda Leib Alter of Ger (1847-1905), also known as the *Sefat Emet*, writes:

> [Abraham and Sarah possessed] the quality of equanimity . . . It is a very great quality for a person to remain whole despite all that happens . . . Most people are not like this; they go through several changes [of heart] every day. But all the changing winds of the world could not shake Abraham and Sarah's equanimity.[3]

The *Sefat Emet* wants us to aspire to this equanimity. If we anchor our sense of well-being to things going our way, then whenever life does not go our way, we face the certainty of becoming unmoored. As an ordinary person, this happens to me many times a day, often trivially: The car ahead of me is not following my orders and is driving too slowly, or the furnace breaks down and I have to toss out all of my plans to get it repaired. How much more do I risk losing my bearings when real losses assault me in my life, as they inevitably do.

Accepting whatever life throws at you is not passivity. It is a supremely active stance, filled with strength and readiness and responsiveness.

These two very different readings—one of Sarah unable to continue, the other praising her equanimity—both point us to the same teaching: It's hard to be a human being, and we are constantly tested by life. Life is fundamentally risky, and this uncertainty can break a person down. But life

---

3. Arthur Green, *The Language of Truth: The Torah Commentary of the Sefat Emet*, p. 35-36, my free rendering.

is also a magnificent journey if we can accept it on its own terms. May we each have the courage and the clarity to live in the company of this paradox, embracing life even as we are willing to let it go.

6

Toldot | תולדות

Isaac Digs His Father's Wells Anew

וְאֵלֶּה תּוֹלְדֹת יִצְחָק בֶּן־אַבְרָהָם אַבְרָהָם הוֹלִיד אֶת־יִצְחָק:

*V'eileh toldot Yitzkhak ben Avraham: Avraham holid
et Yitzkhak.*

These are the generations of Isaac son of Abraham: Abraham
begot Isaac (Genesis 25:19).

THERE ARE TWO *PARASHIYOT* (weekly Torah portions) that begin with
the same wording. *Parashat No'akh* (the portion *"Noah"*) begins "These
are the generations of Noah" (Genesis 6:9). *Parashat Toldot* (the portion
"Toldot" or "Generations") begins "These are the generations of Isaac."

If *Parashat No'akh* is named after its protagonist Noah, why isn't
Parashat Toldot named after its protagonist Isaac? Why is it called *Parashat
Toldot,* and not *Parashat Yitzkhak?*[1]

I assume that our sages were quite intentional in choosing and naming the weekly portions, and that these choices are deeply evocative. They
chose to name this portion "Generations" and not "Isaac." Why?

---

1. My thanks to Bob Messing for raising this stimulating question.

Our first clue to an answer lies in the unusual repetition in our portion's opening verse: "These are the generations of Isaac son of Abraham: Abraham begot Isaac." The first thing the Torah wants to make abundantly clear is that Isaac was Abraham's son. A generational theme is immediately established. Perhaps this portion has something to teach us about the legacy that one generation passes on to the next. And Isaac certainly carries a complex legacy as the son of Abraham. He is the beloved miracle child of his parents' old age, as well as the bearer of the promise God made to them that their descendants would be a blessing to the world. His father Abraham has bequeathed to him a relationship with the God of Creation. And yet, his father also nearly sacrificed Isaac on the altar of his own passionate calling.

As with every legacy we receive from our parents and from the chain of ancestors that preceded them, the good and the bad, the meaningful and the difficult, the traumatic and the life-giving are entwined and entangled. A major portion of our challenge on our respective journeys through life is the work of understanding and coming to terms with the legacy of the generations that preceded us. We are tasked with healing from the traumas that were willy-nilly inflicted upon us while figuring out what parts of that legacy we want to integrate into our own lives and pass on to the next generation.

This reading of Isaac's journey is reinforced by a fascinating passage in the next chapter, 26:15–25: "And the Philistines stopped up all the wells dug by Isaac's father Abraham, filling them with rubble . . . Isaac then began to dig anew the wells that had been dug [by] his father Abraham . . . And when Isaac's servants dug in the wadi, they discovered there a well of living waters!"

One of the names for God in the Torah is מְקוֹר מַיִם חַיִּים *Mekor Mayim Hayim*—the Source of Living Waters. In the Jewish tradition, underground aquifers are a metaphor for the infinite fullness of life that, though unseen, is always flowing beneath the surface of our finite lives. In order to tap that flow and be sustained by it, we must dig down, remove the rubble that impedes our connection to it and create openings so that those ever-present living waters can "well up" to the surface. Then we are able to drink from those waters and sustain others as well. Our ongoing work is to tend those wells, to be those wells. We are the channels through which flow the hidden living waters of life. We can become stopped up in so many ways—pain, fear, despair, fatigue, trauma—and our holy, beautiful work is to keep the well of living waters flowing.

But we are mistaken if we think that we dig our wells from scratch, that we have invented ourselves. We are all, like Isaac, the inheritors of our parents' wells.

And clearing the rubble from this central and formative relationship of our lives requires great perseverance. The story of Isaac's digging hints at this arduous process. The first well that Isaac's servants dig, Isaac names עֵשֶׂק *Eisek*, which means "Quarrel." The second well Isaac names שִׂטְנָה *Sitnah*, "Animosity" or "Accusation." Only when the third well is dug is there no quarrel or animosity, and Isaac names that well רְחֹבוֹת *Rekhovot*, "Spaciousness." As I look back on my engagement with my parents' legacy, I remember a long process of wrangling and resenting and accusing. But I kept digging and eventually found Spaciousness—an acceptance and embrace of both the fierce, abiding love and the *mishegas* that my parents bequeathed to me. I intend to keep tending this well, which is now mine, so that hopefully, I leave a minimum of unnecessary rubble for my children to clear out. They will have enough of their own!

I am also the inheritor of Judaism's wells. The older I get, the more my awe and respect grows for all the Jews who came before me and kept those wells open against almost unfathomable hardship and odds. I faithfully continue to excavate the rubble of pain and trauma that keeps threatening to stop up these wells, so that the life-giving beauty of Judaism can continue to flow into the world. I do it not only for myself, even though I am the grateful beneficiary of Judaism's sustaining teachings. I do it for the sake of the generations that came before me and for the generations that will hopefully follow, that they may continue to dig these wells anew and drink from the living waters.

One final teaching: The Baal Shem Tov, the founder of Hasidism, was asked why the *Amidah*, the central prayer of the daily service, begins with "God of Abraham, God of Isaac, God of Jacob" (and we add, "God of Sarah, God of Rebecca, God of Rachel, God of Leah"). Isn't this redundant? Why not just say "God of Abraham, Isaac and Jacob (Sarah, Rebecca, Rachel and Leah)"? The Baal Shem Tov answered: "The God of Jacob was not the God of Isaac, and the God of Isaac was not the God of Abraham. Each grasped God in his own way, and so must each of us. Only then will God's presence continue to dwell in this world."

Isaac dug his father's wells anew. He made them his own. He named them. He drank from them. We cannot passively accept previous generations' ideas about religion or God—any more than we can passively accept our parents' legacy to us—and expect the living waters to continue to fill the well of our lives. The very survival of those legacies depends upon us claiming them as our own. It is another paradox; we cannot become our authentic, autonomous selves until we also fully embrace our place in the chain of generations. Rabbi Avraham Yitzkhak Kook expressed it thus, "What is old shall be made new, and what is new shall be made holy."

Like Isaac, we have a lot of digging to do. But let's not think of it as drudgery; rather, let's sing this song while we work: וּשְׁאַבְתֶּם־מַיִם בְּשָׂשׂוֹן מִמַּעַיְנֵי הַיְשׁוּעָה *U'shavtem mayim b'sasson, mima'ynei ha'yeshuah*—"Draw water in joy from the living well!" (Isaiah 12:3).

7 ———————————————

Vayeitzei | ויצא

This Is The Place

וַיֵּצֵא יַעֲקֹב מִבְּאֵר שָׁבַע וַיֵּלֶךְ חָרָנָה: וַיִּפְגַּע בַּמָּקוֹם וַיָּלֶן שָׁם

Va'yeitzei Ya'akov miBe'eir Shava va'yeilekh Haranah.
Va'yifga bamakom va'yalen sham

And Jacob left Be'er Sheva and set out for Haran. He encountered The Place, and he spent the night there (Genesis
28:10–11).

THIS IS THE BEGINNING of Jacob's journey of spiritual awakening. By
impersonating his brother Esau, Jacob had tricked his blind father, Isaac,
and acquired the special blessing of the firstborn intended for Esau. But
now, Esau wants to kill him, and Jacob has been forced to run away from
the only home he has ever known. Jacob is alone, perhaps for the first time
in his life. Jacob has acquired his brother's blessing, but he does not know
what his own blessing might be. Since the womb, Jacob has been wrestling
with his twin brother, Esau, trying to surpass him. Jacob's name, *Ya'akov*,
even means tailing or following. Now, Jacob has achieved the goal of his
young life: He has surpassed his brother. By impersonating Esau, Jacob has
even become, in a way, Esau. But who is Jacob? Jacob doesn't know. The

journey he has now been forced to take will be a journey of self-discovery. It will be long and challenging, and Jacob will have to face the consequences of his previous deceits. Ultimately, Jacob will be ready to return home, and he will acquire a new name as a mark of his transformation: Israel.

But that is in the future. Right now, Jacob is alone, frightened perhaps, having no idea what lies ahead. His world has been shattered. But sometimes, the broken vessel of one's life is precisely what allows new insight to shine through. The Torah tells us that upon leaving home, Jacob then "encountered The Place." The Hebrew is unusual here. The Torah could simply read—וַיָּבוֹא אֶל מָקוֹם וַיָּלֶן שָׁם *Va'yavo el makom va'yalen sham*— "He came to a place and spent the night there." Instead, the Torah says *Va'yifga bamakom. Va'yifga* is a very active verb; he "engaged," he "encountered." *Bamakom* means "The Place," not merely a place. Our Torah, a book of visions and dreams in which every encounter is packed with meaning, wants us to take notice; something profound might happen here, if Jacob is ready for it.

> And he lay down in The Place, and he dreamed, and here! A ladder was set on the ground with its top reaching to heaven, and here! Angels of God going up and coming down on it, and here! YHVH stood over him and said, "I am YHVH, God of your father Abraham and Isaac . . ." (Genesis 28:11–13).

When Jacob wakes up, he declares, "Truly, God is in this place, and I was not aware of it! How awesome is this place! This is none other than the house of God and the gateway to heaven!" (Genesis 28:16–17). This is not just awakening from a dream; this is Jacob's spiritual awakening.

Where is this Place where one can become aware of and astonished by the awesome presence of the Infinite? Our tradition reads it on two levels. On the one hand, the place is Mount Moriah, the future site of the Holy Temple in Jerusalem. This is the very same mountaintop on which Abraham bound Isaac. It is the *axis mundi*—the cosmic axis, the holy pinnacle where heaven and earth touch. And so, for thousands of years, we have journeyed up to Jerusalem on pilgrimages to the holy mountain to encounter The Place where God dwells.

On the other hand, Jewish tradition understands that if God's energy is everywhere, then it is possible to encounter God anywhere. That is, any place can be The Place where we meet God. In fact, our sages declare that

הַמָּקוֹם *Hamakom*, The Place, is one of the names of God.[1] Whenever we awaken to the wonder of any given moment, we tremble like Jacob at the awesome awareness of being here in this world at this moment. As I pause for a moment from writing, I see yesterday's snowfall out my window, I feel the warmth from the radiator near my desk, and the cascade of marvels once again overwhelms me: God is in this place, and for the umpteenth time, I had lapsed out of awareness of this abiding truth. How awesome is this Place! It is the House of God; I dwell in the House of God.

Now Jacob is aware that he is not alone—that he is, in fact, always accompanied by and immersed in a great symphony of Being. He has for the first time transcended his callow self-absorption and is awash in humble wonder. This is the true beginning of his journey towards full selfhood and towards becoming a mensch.

At this moment, as you read these words, may you pause and notice that the place you are at this moment is The Place. A ladder connecting heaven and earth stands right before you. Climb up a few rungs and enjoy the view, and hold that wondrous feeling with you as you journey on. You are not alone.

---

1. The verse cited at the beginning of this essay reads *Vayifga Bamakom. Bamakom* means "at the place" and follows the rules of Hebrew grammar. The intended meaning of *Bamakom* and *Hamakom* are the same.

8 ———————————————————

Vayishlakh | וישלח

What's in a Name?

וַיֹּאמֶר לֹא יַעֲקֹב יֵאָמֵר עוֹד שִׁמְךָ כִּי אִם־יִשְׂרָאֵל כִּי־שָׂרִיתָ
עִם־אֱלֹהִים וְעִם־אֲנָשִׁים וַתּוּכָל:

*Va'yomer, "Lo Ya'akov yei'ameir od shimkha, ki im
Yisrael, ki sarita im Elohim v'im anashim va'tukhal."*

And he said, "No more shall you be called Jacob, but Israel,
for you have struggled with God and with men, and you have
overcome" (Genesis 32:29).

I LOVE THIS STORY.

It's time for Jacob to go home and face his past. It has been 20 years
since he stole his brother Esau's blessing and then had to run for his life.
Jacob fled with nothing, and now, 20 years later, he returns with a family,
flocks and herds. He sends messengers ahead to tell Esau that his brother
Jacob has returned, and the messengers return to tell Jacob that his brother
Esau is indeed coming to meet him, along with 400 men!

Jacob is terrified. He assumes that Esau is coming to fulfill his old
promise to kill him. Always the plotter, Jacob sends many gifts ahead to
his brother in the hope of appeasing him, and he splits his family into two

separate camps to protect at least some of them. Jacob is left alone at night by the riverbank.

All night long an unnamed man (we assume he is an angel, a Divine messenger, even though the biblical text never confirms the man's identity) wrestles with Jacob. Jacob's hip is wrenched, but he will not succumb. As dawn is breaking, the angel insists on being released, but Jacob will not let him go until he bestows a blessing on Jacob. The angel blesses Jacob with a new name, יִשְׂרָאֵל *Yisrael*, Israel, meaning, as the angel says, "you have wrestled with God and with men and you have overcome."

Now the sun climbs over the horizon and shines on Jacob (now Israel) as he limps towards his brother, Esau. Israel carries no weapons and no guile. For the first time in his life, he is not scheming or competing with his brother—not trying to get whatever it is that his brother has. He knows that he must face Esau and accept the consequences of his past actions, even if that means his own death.

Jacob's transformation is reflected in his change of names. In the womb, he and Esau wrestle for predominance. The Torah tells us that Jacob emerged second, holding on to his brother's עָקֵב *eikev*, his heel, and so they name him יַעֲקֹב *Ya'akov*, "heel-holder," perhaps. But עָקֵב *eikev* in Hebrew bears multiple associations, very similar to the word "heel" in English. As verbs, both "heel" and *eikev* mean to follow closely; since Jacob emerged right behind Esau, holding his heel, that meaning is probably implied as well. And when we call someone a "heel," we mean that person is devious and untrustworthy. The same in Hebrew: *Eikev* can also mean "crooked." In Jacob's early life, all of his actions were devious, as he was consumed by his desire to supplant Esau as the firstborn.

All those formative years, he wrestled with his brother. Only now is he ready to encounter him face to face. After 20 years away, יַעֲקֹב *Ya'akov* the heel is finally ready to wrestle with his own past actions, his inner nature and his fear. He merits the new name יִשְׂרָאֵל *Yisrael*, God-wrestler. But *Yisrael* also echoes the multiple meanings of *Ya'akov*; Jacob's new name can also be read as יָשָׁר אֵל *Yashar El*—"God is the straight path (meaning honorable, or upright)." I think this is an intentional echo of a famous saying of Isaiah: וְהָיָה הֶעָקֹב לְמִישׁוֹר *V'haya ha'akov l'mishor*—"and the crooked shall be made straight . . . [and the glory of YHVH will be revealed, and all people will see it together]" (Isaiah 40:4-5).

Jacob's new awareness—let's call it *Yisrael*-consciousness—will falter many times during his long life, but at this moment, Jacob truly is *Yisrael*.

As the sunlight supplants the long night and pours down on the transformed Jacob, Esau runs to meet him, embraces and kisses him, and they weep together.

As they speak, Jacob appeals to Esau to accept the blessing that Jacob had stolen from him so long ago. Esau demurs, "I have plenty, my brother, you keep it." But Jacob insists, "Please accept my blessing, for God has been gracious to me, and I have everything." For the first time, Jacob understands that he is indeed blessed, that his life is sufficient, that he has all that he needs. He doesn't need what his brother has and perhaps never did. Jacob gazes wondrously at Esau and says, "Seeing your face is like seeing the face of God."

A precious moment: One could say that Jacob, in his entire life, had never looked at Esau directly. Esau had always been only an obstacle for Jacob to surmount. Jacob had never actually met his brother's gaze and understood that Esau, too, was a child of God. But now, Jacob had spent the night wrestling with his own fears, his own projections and his own history of manipulating his brother for his own gain. Jacob faced all this and did not succumb. His going out to meet Esau is a heroic moment, in which the hero knows that he must face his own death in order to become the person he was meant to be. As a result of rising to this occasion, our hero Jacob—now transformed and no longer a heel, now upright and no longer crooked—merits a new name: Israel. And Israel is able to see for the first time the Divine imprint in the face of Esau, his lifelong nemesis.

This is one of the key episodes in our Torah because it recounts the story of "How We Received Our Name." We are the Children of Israel, and this is where we learn the meaning of our name. I compare this story in importance to the Passover story in the book of Exodus, which tells us "How We Became a People." They are both origin myths, stories that tell us who we are, how we came to be and what we are meant to become. The Exodus story teaches us that we were slaves and became a free people, and that this identity should ever inform our sensitivity to the powerless and the oppressed.

And what might the story of Jacob's transformation into Israel teach us about what it means to be one of the "Children of Israel," the God-Wrestler? How do we merit this transformational name? What must each of us face and wrestle with in order to be a member of this clan?

To be a descendant of Israel is to wrestle with life, to struggle with life's deeper meaning and purpose, to not succumb to despair or confusion or fear.

To be a descendant of Israel is to understand that we are responsible for our actions, and that our past will haunt us and cripple us if we do not face and wrestle with our demons.

To be a descendant of Israel is to be willing to have all the crooked paths of old habits and defenses and justifications die, so that we can face life and one another directly, humbly and courageously.

9 ———————————————

Vayeishev | וישב

What Goes Down Must Come Up!

וַיֵּשֶׁב יַעֲקֹב בְּאֶרֶץ מְגוּרֵי אָבִיו בְּאֶרֶץ כְּנָעַן: אֵלֶּה תֹּלְדוֹת יַעֲקֹב
יוֹסֵף בֶּן־שְׁבַע־עֶשְׂרֵה שָׁנָה הָיָה רֹעֶה אֶת־אֶחָיו בַּצֹּאן

Va'yeishev Ya'akov b'eretz m'gurei aviv b'eretz kna'an.
Eileh toldot Ya'akov: Yosef ben sh'va esrei shanah
hayah ro'eh et ekhav batzon

Jacob now settled in the land of his father's sojourning, in the
land of Canaan. These are the generations of Jacob: Joseph
was seventeen years old, and he would tend the flocks with
his brothers (Genesis 37:1–2).

AFTER MANY JOURNEYS, JACOB finally settles down. He will live on
for many more years, but the narrative focus now shifts to his children's
generation, specifically to his favorite son, Joseph. The life of Joseph drives
our story through the remainder of the book of Genesis.

Joseph is an amazingly rich character, encompassing qualities of arrogance and humility, betrayal and reconciliation, memory and trauma,
the power of dreams and the way we create meaning out of our complicated lives. Joseph's life is at the fulcrum of multiple narrative threads in

the Torah reaching back to Cain and Abel, and ahead through the Exodus from Egypt. Joseph's saga, though only 13 magnificently crafted chapters in the Torah, has epic proportions; Thomas Mann's masterpiece *Joseph and His Brothers*, which expands on the biblical narrative (and which I truly hope to read some day), covers 1,492 pages!

Here I will focus on just one of the themes in Joseph's story: the ups and downs of life. Joseph's life is a roller coaster. He is his father's favorite, wearing a special coat of many colors. His brothers throw him down into a pit as they debate whether or not to kill him. They haul him up and sell him to traders, who bring him down to Egypt as a slave: וְיוֹסֵף הוּרַד מִצְרָיְמָה *V'Yosef hurad Mitzraimah*—Now Joseph was brought down to Egypt (Genesis 39:1). Joseph rises up to be the steward of his master Potiphar's household. But when he refuses the advances of Potiphar's wife, he is sent down to the dungeon. Two years later, he is summoned to interpret Pharaoh's dreams, and he rises to become the vizier of Egypt.

Many years later, Joseph's brothers bow before him as supplicants, begging for food, not knowing that this potentate is their long-lost brother. When Joseph reveals his identity to them, they fear for their lives and await revenge. But to their astonishment, Joseph reassures them: "Don't be troubled that you sold me here, for it was to save lives that God sent me ahead of you" (Genesis 45:5).

Joseph could be understandably bitter about the trajectory of his life: cast out of his family, repeatedly betrayed, imprisoned despite his innocence. He could easily view himself as a self-made man, surviving on his wits and with no allegiance other than to his own survival. But that is not the lesson Joseph has gleaned from the descents and ascents of his turbulent life. Instead, Joseph sees the "downs" as necessary precursors to the "ups."

The Hasidic masters coined a term for this perspective on life: יְרִידָה לְצֹרֶךְ עֲלִיָה *yeridah l'tzorekh aliyah*—"a descent that facilitates an ascent." Jewish spiritual wisdom understands this phenomenon as intrinsic to our life here on earth. We all have setbacks in our lives; much happens to us over which we have no control and against which we must struggle, and that struggle can strengthen and ennoble us. We make poor choices, and then must recover and learn from them. We learn compassion for others by experiencing suffering ourselves. There is no rising without falling.

Mark Twain put it this way: "Good judgment is the result of experience and experience the result of bad judgment."

I don't share this glibly. Many times, the "downs" take us so low, and into such darkness and suffering that we cannot rise up again. Life is not an amusement park ride; there are no seatbelts and no guarantees. Yet at the same time, we cannot gain in awareness, experience, faith or love unless we view the problems and setbacks in our lives as opportunities to learn and grow.

Jewish mystical teaching sees *yeridah l'tzorekh aliyah* as intrinsic not only to human life, but also to the entire pattern of creation. That is, the Divine light descended, or contracted itself, into physical form and inheres within every atom of the universe.

The nature of those Divine sparks is that they yearn to be liberated and restored to their infinite Source. For the mystic, this cosmic process is inevitable: What goes down must come up! But we humans, having been granted free choice, have the capacity to either ignore or to participate in this process, to hinder or to hasten the revelation of the light. Our holy task as partners in the process of Life Unfolding is to discern the holy sparks hidden everywhere in creation, especially within ourselves and within other people, to fan their flames with our love and to let those little lights shine. (*Vayeishev* is always read right before Hanukkah, and I feel a Hanukkah teaching coming on here!)

In the course of his roller-coaster life, Joseph gained a growing awareness that the downs were a necessary precondition for the ups that would follow. Joseph embraced his entire life—the downs as well as the ups—as inextricably linked. There was no episode that did not teach him. Every chapter contributed to making him the person he had become. In some inexplicable way, he was grateful for it all. So may it be for us.

10 —————————————————

Mikeitz | מקץ

Sparks of Light in a Broken World—
In Memory of Leonard Cohen

וַיַּרְא יַעֲקֹב כִּי יֶשׁ־שֶׁבֶר בְּמִצְרָיִם

Va'yar Ya'akov ki yesh shever b'Mitzrayim

And Jacob saw that there was grain in Egypt (Genesis 42:1).

WE LOST A SAGE of our era with Leonard Cohen's passing. His absence prompted me, as it has so many others, to revisit his words and to absorb his unflinching wisdom. Leonard Cohen was a prophet of brokenness, a seeker of the light who did not ignore the inherent frailties and folly of the human condition. In *"Anthem"* (1992), he sang:

> Ring the bells that still can ring
> Forget your perfect offering
> There is a crack in everything
> That's how the light gets in.

These words echo the teachings of Jewish mysticism. Rabbi Isaac Luria, a formative giant of *Kabbalah* who lived and taught in Tzfat (Safed) in the mountains of the Galilee in the 16th century, explained the brokenness of our world with a compelling origin story that still animates Jewish thinking today. Luria explained that when God attempted to create our world, God poured the infinite Divine light into the vessel of creation. But it was impossible for the finite creation to contain that infinite light. The light caused the vessel of creation to crack. Much of the light escaped and rejoined the Divine source, but much also remained hidden in the shards of our sublime yet broken world.

Luria taught that the human task is to find and recognize the countless sparks of Divine light. Through our attention and devotion to freeing these sparks, we do our part in helping to repair the broken vessel of our world. Luria named this process תִּקוּן עוֹלָם *Tikkun Olam*, "Repairing the World."

So we can see the *Kabbalistic* background of Leonard Cohen's verse, but what has this got to do with our Torah portion? As Jacob addresses his sons at the beginning of Chapter 42, there is a vast famine underway. Unbeknown to Jacob, his son Joseph is in Egypt. Joseph successfully interpreted Pharaoh's dreams as predicting seven years of plenty, followed by seven years of famine; he then proposed a plan to store the grain of the plentiful years in preparation for the lean years to come. Joseph is now second-in-command to Pharaoh, disbursing that grain to feed the entire populace. News travels to Canaan about the food stores in Egypt, "And Jacob saw that there was grain in Egypt."— *Va'yar Ya'akov ki yesh shever b'Mitzrayim.* Jacob will send his sons down to Egypt to procure provisions, thus setting into motion the drama of their reunion with Joseph.

Rabbi Menachem Nachum of Chernobyl, known by his pen name *Me'or Eiynayim*, "Enlightener of the Eyes," was a disciple of the Ba'al Shem Tov and a Hasidic master of the 18th century. Rabbi Menachem Nachum offers a mystical interpretation of this verse. Remember, Jewish spiritual teachers throughout the ages understand Torah as primarily a spiritual rather than a physical journey. Rabbi Menachem Nachum notices that שֶׁבֶר *shever*, which means "grain" or "provisions," also means "brokenness" or "breakage." He also notes that מִצְרַיִם *Mitzrayim*, which means "Egypt," also means "the narrow place" or "constriction." Thus, he reads the verse *Va'yar Ya'akov ki yesh shever b'Mitzrayim* as "And Jacob saw that there was brokenness in the Place of Constriction."

On the spiritual journey, *Mitzrayim* is our physical world: a place of constriction and brokenness, in which the Divine Light is present but hidden. Our task as spiritual beings is to descend from the Promised Land, the place of Divine Oneness, into the world of broken vessels—vessels that were shattered when the light of Oneness overflowed into them. The task of Jacob's sons—that is, the Children of Israel—is to recognize the sparks of light that are hidden and waiting to be released, and uplifted by our searching hearts and our righteous deeds.

Father Jacob sees the light glimmering through the cracks of our shattered world. He sends us down into our beautiful, broken world to seek that light in all we do, and to liberate the sparks and let them fly! Rarely is that a simple or easy task, but who said that a life filled with purpose was supposed to be easy? May we be blessed with each other's good company as we pursue our holy, human work.

The light is always there, mingled with dark, but we have to know where to look and how to see. Or as Leonard Cohen—Eliezer ben Natan ha'Cohen was his Jewish name—taught us in *"Suzanne"*:

> And she shows you where to look amid the garbage and the flowers
> There are heroes in the seaweed, there are children in the morning
> They are leaning out for love and they will lean that way forever

His memory is a blessing.

Parashat Mikeitz always falls during Hanukkah. May the light of the Hanukkah flames remind us of the light shining through the cracks of our broken and beautiful world, and in the coming year, may we know where to look amid the garbage and the flowers.

11

Vayigash | ויגש

Judah and Joseph

וַיִּגַּשׁ אֵלָיו יְהוּדָה וַיֹּאמֶר בִּי אֲדֹנִי . . .

Va'yigash eilav Yehudah va'yomer "Bi Adoni . . ."

And Judah approached him and said, "By your leave, my
Lord . . ." (Genesis 44:18).

THIS MAY BE THE most dramatic moment in the entire book of Genesis.
During the long famine, 10 of Joseph's brothers had come down to Egypt to
seek provisions. Joseph, now vizier of Egypt and in charge of food distribu-
tion, recognized his brothers, but they did not recognize him. The last time
they had seen Joseph was when they sold him into slavery 20 years ago, and
there is no reason that they would identify the potentate before whom they
now bow as their long-lost brother.

Joseph does not trust his brothers. He tests them mercilessly to ascer-
tain whether or not they have changed since their nearly murderous betrayal. He insists that they bring his younger brother Benjamin with them
to Egypt, although Jacob protests. Benjamin and Joseph are the two sons of
Jacob's beloved late wife, Rachel. Jacob has been grieving the loss of Joseph
all these years, while doing everything he could to keep Benjamin safe and

nearby. If Jacob loses Benjamin as he did Joseph, Jacob may very well die of grief. But famine looms, and Jacob relinquishes Benjamin to Egypt so that they all might avert starvation. When the brothers arrive with Benjamin to Joseph's court, Joseph can barely control himself, and he excuses himself and weeps privately upon seeing his long-lost brother. But Joseph then once again dons his public face, and continues to test and torment his clueless brothers; he frames Benjamin with a crime and blithely tells the other brothers that they can go home in peace—only the guilty party, Benjamin, will remain in servitude in Egypt.

What are the brothers to do? Will they once again abandon their kin? Will they once again dissemble to their father about their actions, as when they faked Joseph's death 20 years earlier? They still carry the guilt of that betrayal. Unaware that Joseph understood their conversation, the brothers had earlier said to one another, "Alas, we are guilty for what we did to our brother Joseph! We saw his distress when he pleaded with us those many years ago, but we did not listen." Reuben then chastised his brothers, "Didn't I tell you back then not to sin against the lad Joseph? But you wouldn't listen, and now our guilt has come due!" (Genesis 42:20–21).

At this critical moment, this week's Torah portion begins. Judah musters all of his integrity and all of his courage, and steps forward: "*Va'yigash eilav Yehuda*—And Judah approached him." Judah makes an impassioned, extended plea for Benjamin's release, finally offering his own life in place of Benjamin's. Somehow, Judah reaches into Joseph: "Joseph could no longer restrain himself . . . He cried aloud . . . then said to his brothers, 'I am Joseph! Is my father truly still alive?'" (Genesis 44:1–3).

The dam has broken. Joseph removes his mask and pours out his feelings. Reconciliation is now possible, and the family will be reunited.

Torah commentators throughout the ages have elaborated on how Judah accomplished this breakthrough. One *midrash* focuses on the multiple shades of the term *va'yigash*, "he approached." The *midrash* scans the Torah for all the places where the term *va'yigash* is employed and discovers that in different contexts one can approach to make peace, to do battle or to pray. Therefore, the *midrash* proposes that Judah approached Joseph ready for any possible outcome: He was prepared to appease, to argue or to plead. I think the *midrash* is trying to tell us that Judah stepped forward with no preconceived agenda other than to connect with Joseph. Whatever that would take, Judah was prepared to do. Judah was not concerned for his own pride or physical safety, and his genuineness unlocked Joseph's heart.[1]

Another remarkable *midrash* gives us this image:

> The designs in a person's mind are deep waters, but a person of understanding can draw them out (Proverbs 20:5). "The designs in a person's mind" refers to Joseph; "a person of understanding" refers to Judah. What does this resemble? A deep pit into which no one could climb down. Then a wise person came and brought a long rope that reached down to the water so he could draw from it. So was Joseph deep in the pit, and Judah came and drew him out.[2]

Playing on Joseph's memory of his brothers casting him into a pit when he was a boy, this *midrash* now sees Joseph as traumatized and metaphorically still inaccessible in that deep hole—stuck in the past even though he was physically lifted out many years ago. In this reading, Joseph does not know how to climb out of his psychic pain. The trials through which he puts his brothers are the distress flags that he, perhaps unconsciously, hopes will be recognized. Judah, with his passionate and selfless approach to Joseph, reaches deep down into Joseph's frozen pain and draws it up into the light, where it can begin to dissolve: "And Joseph could no longer restrain himself . . ."

Why was Judah capable of this transformative approach? I think because Judah himself had been transformed by his own journey of loss in his life. We learn this tale in Chapter 38. At first glance, this chapter seems like an odd intrusion into the Joseph story, but we come to understand that it is necessary so that we might understand Judah's development as a person. Judah has three sons. He marries the eldest off to Tamar, and this son dies suddenly. Then, according to the requirement of ancient law, Judah gives his second son to Tamar, but he, too, dies unexpectedly. Judah, now left with only one son, refuses to give him in marriage to Tamar, leaving her in a terrible limbo, unable to marry again. As a result, Judah treats his daughter-in-law Tamar with dismissive contempt.

As that story unfolds, thanks to Tamar's cleverness, Judah is forced to confront his own immoral behavior and make restitution to her. He is finally able to own his callowness, and grow into a moral and empathetic man. We witness this growth in Judah when we compare his behavior when

---

1. *Bereishit Rabbah* 93:4, cited in Aviva Zornberg's magnificent *Genesis: The Beginning of Desire*, p. 318.

2. *Tanchuma Yashan* 2, Zornberg, p. 322

he and his brothers threw Joseph into a pit, and then sold him as a slave, to the way Judah comes to Benjamin's defense in our episode. Twenty years earlier, Judah had torn Joseph's coat of many colors and stained it with goat's blood. Then he blithely showed the coat to his father, who concluded that Joseph had been torn by wild beasts.

In faking Joseph's death, the younger Judah had no idea of the pain he was causing Jacob. As is true about so much of our lives, Judah had to experience tragedy and grief himself in order to understand the grief of his father. Now, 20 years later, Judah understands the pain of losing a child. With Benjamin's life in the balance, Judah knew that he could not cause his father such pain ever again. Judah was even willing to offer himself in Benjamin's stead. Judah could reach down into Joseph's pit because he knew the depths of parental grief and loss from personal experience.

Judah understood that the fragility and the pain that accompany every single human life is true for everyone. Whether potentate or pauper, we are all someone's child; we all yearn for the love that we have lost. At the dramatic moment when Judah approaches the throne, he is no longer intimidated by the fearsome vizier of Egypt, but instead is approaching another human being as an equal. Judah will be heard—and damn the consequences of talking back to the potentate.

The Hasidic teacher the Sefat Emet elaborates on this idea with an ingenious wordplay. The Torah reads, "And Judah approached him and said, בִּי אֲדֹנִי *Bi Adoni*—'By your leave, my Lord . . . ' " Quoting the great *kabbalist* Isaac Luria, the Sefat Emet points out that you could also read that phrase as בִּי אֲדֹנָי *Bi Adonai*, which transforms Judah's statement to mean, "And Judah approached him and said, 'God is within me.' "[3] The wordplay is further amplified by Judah's name in Hebrew: יהודה YHVDH. Embedded within Judah's actual name is the name of God, יהוה YHVH!

Each and every one of us is animated by a Divine spark; each and every one of us is a child of God. No earthly throne or pomp should disguise this truth. At this fateful moment, Judah is aware that he, too, is a child of God; God is in him. Aware of his true status, he approaches Joseph, the vizier of Egypt, without fear. And confronted with Judah's full and courageous humanity, Joseph remembers his own full and courageous humanity. External appearances are abandoned, and two souls can finally meet with their pain and hope and longing expressed.

3. See Arthur Green, *The Language of Truth: The Torah Commentary of the Sefat Emet; Rabbi Yehudah Leib Alter of Ger*, pp. 67–69.

May we all be courageous like Judah, willing to take the risk of sharing our full humanity for the sake of the people we love.

12 ——————

Vay'khi | ויחי

When Torah and Life Intersect

וַיִּקְרְבוּ יְמֵי־יִשְׂרָאֵל לָמוּת . . .

Vayik'revu y'mei Yisrael lamut . . .

When Israel's time to die drew near . . . (Genesis 47:29).

וַיִּקְרְבוּ יְמֵי־דָוִד לָמוּת . . .

Vayik'revu y'mei David lamut . . .

When David's time to die drew near . . . (Haftarah of *Vay'khi,* I Kings 2:1).

THIS *PARASHAH* MARKS THE *yahrzeit* (anniversary of the death) of my father, Dr. David Kligler, of blessed memory. He passed away on the 10th of Tevet 5740, which corresponded that year with Dec. 30, 1979. In Jewish practice, when remembering a loved one, especially a parent, it is customary to honor their memory by teaching some Torah in their name. I wish to remember my father by sharing the story of the mysterious way our lives and family history intersected and merged with the Torah reading of that week: *Parashat Vay'khi*, the closing chapters of the book of Genesis.

My father's father was Professor Israel Jacob Kligler. He came to the United States from Eastern Europe as a child at the very end of the 19th century. Young Israel Jacob proved himself a brilliant student and became one of the first Jews to earn a Ph.D. from Columbia University. His field was infectious diseases and public health. A Zionist, by 1920 he had moved to British Mandate Palestine, and his innovative and tireless research proved crucial in the eradication of malaria in the region. My father David was born in Jerusalem in 1926 to Israel Jacob and Helen Kligler.

Israel Jacob did not live to see the creation of the State of Israel, the cause to which he had dedicated his life. He passed away in 1944 and was buried on the Mount of Olives, the most ancient active Jewish cemetery in the world, overlooking his beloved Jerusalem. David was serving in the U.S. army at the time, painfully separated from his father by oceans and a world war. In 1939, the family had moved to New York City for the year in order to maintain their U.S. citizenship. When the war broke out in Europe, David's parents decided that he should remain in New York with his mother until it was safer to travel. Israel Jacob—apparently more wedded to his research than to his wife—returned to his laboratory at the Hebrew University of Jerusalem. The war, of course, did not "blow over." Israel Jacob returned to New York once more in 1942, as he recovered from a heart attack. But then, yet again, he abandoned his son and went back to Palestine. David remained in the United States. He attended college and medical school, and married Deborah. My parents had three sons and built a meaningful life together here in White Plains, N.Y.

But the longing for home, and for his distant father, apparently never left David, who suffered from tormenting depression. In our family, the ancient Jewish longing to return from exile to our homeland mingled inextricably with our father's own longing to be restored to his home and to his own father in Jerusalem. In 1968, just after the Six-Day War, our family traveled to Israel. The Mount of Olives cemetery had been in Jordanian hands for 19 years, and was destroyed and desecrated. David futilely searched for his father Israel Jacob's gravesite. A monument would soon be placed near the gravesite to mark about 40 graves that had been destroyed, including my grandfather's.

In 1979, my older brother Dan and his wife Roberta made *aliyah* to Israel, and on the third night of Hanukkah, their first child, Eitan, was born.

The *bris* was in Jerusalem, and new grandfather David flew over for the occasion. The event somehow left our father feeling deeply fulfilled and complete; back in New York two weeks later, he ended his lifelong suffering and took his own life.

This is the story I want to tell: We were standing on a hillside attending my father's burial at Mount Hebron Cemetery in Flushing, Queens. We looked out at the Van Wyck Expressway, the old World's Fair fairgrounds and Shea Stadium—a New York vista if there ever was one. Our dear friend Cantor Bill Wolff was officiating. In his brief eulogy, Bill pointed us towards the week's Torah reading, *Vay'khi*:

> Jacob lived in the land of Egypt for 17 years . . . When Israel's time to die drew near, he summoned his son Joseph and said to him . . . "When I am laid to rest with my ancestors, carry me out of Egypt and bury me in their burial place [the Cave of Machpelah, near Hebron] . . . Swear to me" . . . When Jacob was done charging his sons, he drew his feet into the bed, breathed his last, and was gathered to his ancestors (Genesis 47:28–31, 49:33).

Bill then pointed us to the Haftarah portion of *Vay'khi*. The Haftarah (or Haftorah) is a passage from the later books of the Hebrew Bible that was long ago selected to accompany each week's Torah portion. The Haftarah is always somehow thematically linked to the Torah portion. The Haftarah of *Vay'khi* is about King David at the end of his life:

> When David's time to die drew near, he charged his son Solomon: I am going the way of all the earth; you must now be strong and show yourself a man, keeping faith with YHVH your God . . . Then David slept with his ancestors, and was buried in the City of David (I Kings 2: 1–3, 10).

The layers of synchronicity we experienced at that moment overwhelmed us. The week's Torah and Haftarah readings brought the deaths of Israel/Jacob and David together, just as we knew that our David's tragic death was intimately connected to his father Israel Jacob's death decades earlier. The patriarch Israel/Jacob made his children swear to carry his remains out of exile and back to the Promised Land—in fact, to the burial cave in Hebron that his grandfather Abraham had purchased, and where Israel/Jacob's father Isaac and mother Rebecca were buried. How strange that we were standing in Mount Hebron cemetery. But rather than looking towards the Jerusalem hills, this Mount Hebron had a view of Shea Stadium! King David was buried in the City of David, which is Jerusalem, and slept there with his ancestors. Wordlessly, we were immediately certain that our David needed to rest in his birthplace Jerusalem with his ancestors. What David Kligler could not realize in his lifetime we at least would allow him now; we would end his painful exile and bury him on the Mount of Olives, so that he could finally be with his father Israel Jacob.

We made arrangements to have David's body flown to Israel. My brother Dan flew home to Israel and went to the Mount of Olives cemetery office to purchase a burial plot. Alas, all of the plots overlooking Jerusalem had been sold, and we would have to settle for a plot on the far side of the hill. But wait: Looking through their files, the cemetery managers found that there already was a plot reserved in the name of Kligler that had never been filled! We didn't know that decades earlier, David's mother, Helen, had reserved her own plot next to her husband, Israel Jacob. Helen had never used it; her wish was to be cremated when she had died. A plot was waiting in the Kligler name, somehow "reserved" for David, so near to his father's original—now destroyed—burial place and in the shadow of the new monument that had since been erected. David is buried there, with his father, where he belongs, and if you visit his grave, you are graced with the most extraordinary view of Jerusalem.

Then David slept with his ancestors and was buried in the City of David.

How blessed my family was during that tragedy to get a glimpse of the usually invisible lines of connection that seem to link us through time and space, and to be offered a clear, almost irrefutable sense of what needed to happen next. How strange the way that moment's Torah reading and our present moment aligned, and how strange that potential stumbling blocks evaporated as we did for David what we knew we must do.

As a rabbi, I have accompanied many families through the portal of death and loss. It is a mysterious time, when the veil between the worlds becomes less opaque. Many mourners have described to me their own wondrous and inexplicable sense that suddenly, there is a meaningful and interconnected pattern to apparently disparate events. What we usually dismiss as coincidence becomes charged with meaning and importance. Is this a psychological coping mechanism, or is it a window into a level of reality to which we are usually oblivious? I will let others argue about that. I'm too busy marveling at it all.

There is yet another synchronous aspect to my father's passing that I wish to add. As I mentioned earlier, my father died on the 10th of Tevet, known in Hebrew as עֲשָׂרָה בְּטֵבֵת *Asara B'Tevet,* the day on which I write these words. *Asara B'Tevet* is a fast day on the Jewish calendar that marks the day Jerusalem was besieged by King Nebuchadnezzar's armies more than 2,500 years ago. For Jews, it is a day of mourning for Jerusalem's destruction and for our subsequent long exile. How strangely fitting that my father had chosen this day to die.

And so, when I mourn for Jerusalem, I mourn for my father David, of blessed memory. When I rejoice for Jerusalem, I rejoice for my father David, of blessed memory. The past and the present, the stories of the Bible, and the stories of my own family intertwine and merge, forever and ever. I am embedded in a blessed mystery. Amen.

שמות
Exodus

והנה הסנה בער באש והסנה איננו אכל

Behold, the bush was burning with fire, but the
bush was not consumed. (Exodus 3:2)

13 ─────────────────────────────

Shemot | שמות

The Long Walk to Freedom

וַיֹּ֙אמֶר֙ מֶ֣לֶךְ מִצְרַ֔יִם לַֽמְיַלְּדֹ֖ת הָֽעִבְרִיֹּ֑ת אֲשֶׁ֨ר שֵׁ֤ם הָֽאַחַת֙ שִׁפְרָ֔ה וְשֵׁ֥ם הַשֵּׁנִ֖ית פּוּעָֽה: וַיֹּ֗אמֶר בְּיַלֶּדְכֶן֙ אֶת־הָֽעִבְרִיֹּ֔ות וּרְאִיתֶ֖ן עַל־הָאׇבְנָ֑יִם אִם־בֵּ֥ן הוּא֙ וַהֲמִתֶּ֣ן אֹתֹ֔ו וְאִם־בַּ֥ת הִ֖וא וָחָֽיָה:

Va'yomer melekh Mitzrayim la'meyaldot ha'ivriyot asher sheim ha'akhat Shifrah v'sheim ha'sheinit Pu'ah va'yomer b'yaldekhen et ha'ivriyot ur'item al ha'ovnayim im bein hu v'hamiten oto v'im bat hi v'khayah.

The king of Egypt spoke to the Hebrew midwives, one of whom was named Shifrah and the other Puah, saying, "When you deliver the Hebrew women, look at the birthstool: if it is a boy, kill him; if it is a girl, let her live (Exodus 1:15–16).

THIS WEEK WE BEGIN the book of Exodus, a book that changed the world. With this story, the Torah introduced a new paradigm to human affairs. Throughout most of human history, kings and emperors have been

51

granted god-like status. The king was unlike other humans, and the king's word was law. The Torah, however, posited a Power in the universe that was greater than any king. (Hence, "King of Kings" becomes one of the names for God in our tradition.) This Power created all human beings in the Divine image, and therefore, early Judaism presented a direct refutation to the concept that any single human being could claim Divine status.

This was a revolutionary concept: No man's word or whim could be law. A moral law transcended even the king's decrees. To dehumanize any person, to treat him or her as less human than oneself, was a desecration of the very essence of creation. The Torah offers a "new world order": kings and tyrants, beware! Every person is a child of God, and as such has infinite value, regardless of station. Do not subject and subvert them to your will for power. Do not reduce them to cogs in your profit machine. (Even though the Torah does not abolish the institution of slavery—this takes place only in modern times—the Torah insists that since slaves are human beings, they must be treated with decency and dignity.)

Our Torah sends a hero, Moses, to carry the message of this great new understanding, and to lead the oppressed to freedom. But Moses's way is prepared by others—specifically, by women.

Shifrah and Puah, the Hebrew midwives, are singled out by name. "The midwives, fearing God, did not do as the king of Egypt had told them; they let the boys live" (Exodus 1:17). Perhaps this is the first recorded act of civil disobedience. In the idiom of the Torah, the midwives acted as they did because they feared God more than they feared the Pharaoh. In our modern idiom, we might say that the midwives revered life more than they feared Pharaoh. Acting according to their conscience and compassion, Shifrah and Puah risked their lives to preserve life.

I especially love that the Torah pits midwives against Pharaoh as the first confrontation against tyranny. Midwives serve life. That Pharaoh would insist that the midwives destroy life highlights his almost total disconnection from this orientation. Pharaoh is the embodiment of self-absorbed egomania. The world exists only for his gratification. Shifrah and Puah's lives are other-centered, dedicated to bringing new life into the world. How could they not revere and be devoted to the wondrous Creator of all? How could they participate in the horror of the king's decree?

Shifrah and Puah cannot defy Pharaoh to his face. He will certainly have them killed. They must resort to the arsenal of the powerless: deception.

The king of Egypt summoned the midwives and said to them, "Why have you done this thing, letting the boys live?" The midwives said to Pharaoh, "Because the Hebrew women are not like the Egyptian women: they are animals. Before we even get there, they have given birth!" (Exodus 1:18–19).

The midwives know that Pharaoh doesn't see the Hebrews as fully human. And so, they play to his bias: "The Hebrew women are like animals, nothing like your civilized Egypt. How can you expect us to control them?"

The oppressive master always convinces himself that his slaves or serfs or victims are less than human. Throughout human history and ubiquitous still, this is the rationale that validates cruelty. But the victims of that cruelty remain resourceful. Despite their lack of overt power, they are experts at survival and know their master's foibles. Shifrah and Puah expertly play Pharaoh.

Moses risks all to confront Pharaoh and lead the slaves to freedom. Moses is a hero. But the "Great Man" theory of historical change is sorely incomplete. Countless acts of anonymous courage and resistance maintain the hidden springs of hope and human dignity, so that they are ready for the moment when justice and righteousness finally begin to roll like a mighty stream. Praise to all the Shifrahs and Puahs throughout history and today—countless resourceful, brave, determined and almost always unsung heroes. Without their courage and wits, we would not be here to tell the tale.

This teaching is dedicated to the blessed memory of Rabbi Abraham Joshua Heschel (1907–1972). His yahrzeit falls on the week of Parashat Shemot. Rabbi Heschel joined his friend, Dr. Martin Luther King Jr., on the march from Selma to Montgomery, and then wrote King saying, "I felt my legs were praying."

14 ———————————————

Va'eira | וארא

I Will Be With You

וַיְדַבֵּר מֹשֶׁה לִפְנֵי יְהוָֹה לֵאמֹר הֵן בְּנֵי־יִשְׂרָאֵל לֹא־שָׁמְעוּ אֵלַי
וְאֵיךְ יִשְׁמָעֵנִי פַרְעֹה וַאֲנִי עֲרַל שְׂפָתָיִם:

*Vay'daber Moshe lifnei YHVH leimor: "Hen B'nei
Yisrael lo sham'u eilai v'eich yishm'eini Phar'oh, va'ani
aral sfatayim!"*

And Moses spoke to YHVH, saying: "Look, the Children of
Israel would not listen to me; how then should Pharaoh listen
to me—me, a man of impeded speech!" (Exodus 6:12).

MOSES, THE RELUCTANT PROPHET, has returned to his home in Egypt
with a seemingly impossible mission. Raised as a prince in Pharaoh's palace,
he had run away many years before and become a shepherd in Midian. In a
life-changing encounter in the wilderness, Moses has a vision of a burning
bush and hears a call from the very heart of existence: "I am YHVH, Life
Unfolding, Being Itself. I have seen the suffering of the slaves in Egypt, and

I know their pain. This is not the purpose for which I created human beings. I will be with you. Go to Pharaoh and tell him to let my people go!"[1]

Moses demurs, thinking of every possible reason that would disqualify him from this mission, but there is no turning back. Moses makes his way to the royal palace and informs Pharaoh that YHVH, the Source of all Being, insists that Pharaoh let the people go. Pharaoh famously replies, "Who is YHVH that I should listen to that voice and let Israel go? I do not know YHVH, nor will I let Israel go" (Exodus 5:2).

In response to this threat, Pharaoh doubles the labors of the slaves, and adds both backbreaking and morale-breaking measures to their daily toil.

As we enter this week's portion, YHVH again gives Moses a message of great hope and charges Moses to relay this message to the slaves:

> I am YHVH, Life Unfolding ... I will rescue you from bondage, and deliver you with an outstretched arm ... and I will be your God, and you will know that it is I, YHVH, Life Unfolding, who liberates you from the burdens of Egypt. And I will bring you to the land I promised to Abraham, Isaac and Jacob as your inheritance. I am YHVH! (Exodus 6:6–8)
>
> But when Moses told this to the Israelites, they could not listen to Moses, their spirits crushed by cruel bondage (Exodus 6:9).

Neither Pharaoh nor the Israelites accept Moses's message. In fact, things have gotten worse since Moses showed up. YHVH then instructs Moses to once again speak to Pharaoh. Moses is beside himself, and says, "Look here, the Children of Israel would not listen to me; how then should Pharaoh listen to me—me, a man of impeded speech!" (Exodus 6:12).

Our story has reached an impasse. Moses carries a message of liberation and hope. Pharaoh will not, perhaps cannot listen—why should he when he is the beneficiary of the status quo? The slaves will not, perhaps cannot listen; they are קְצֶר רוּחַ *kotzer ruakh*, which can either mean "short of breath" or "of crushed spirit." Moses is stymied. No one seems capable of hearing his message.

The Hebrew describes Moses as עֲרַל שְׂפָתָיִם *aral sfatayim*. In the case of circumcision, *aral* means "foreskin." Here, it means that Moses has a foreskin—that is, a sheath over his lips. He is unable to speak. We know from earlier in the narrative that Moses claims to be "slow of speech," but

---

1. Here, I have condensed the lengthy dialogue between YHVH and Moses in Exodus, Chapter 3.

the Torah is trying to say something much more profound than that Moses suffers from a stutter.

The Hasidic master the Sefat Emet guides us into a deeper explanation for Moses's "speech impediment." The Sefat Emet reads Moses's complaint to God as "because neither Pharaoh nor the Children of Israel will listen, therefore I am unable to speak." In other words, it is not the speaker who offers speech; it is the listener who elicits speech. All of us have had this experience and know it to be true. I am sure you can think of a time when you sensed someone's genuine interest in hearing what you had to say, and you found yourself talking much more than you expected to. I'm sure you can think of a time when you turned your loving ear to someone that you cared deeply about and "drew her out of her shell."

Moses can no longer speak because he does not believe his words will make a difference. How does the prophet, the idealist, the messenger of hope and possibility in the midst of misery and despair continue when his or her message appears to fall on deaf ears? How do any of us remember that we have something of value to communicate when it seems that no one cares? At this nadir of hope, where will Moses find the strength to continue to speak?

The answer can be found back in Moses's encounter with YHVH at the burning bush: Moses said to God, "Who am I that I should go to Pharaoh and free the Israelites from Egypt? And God said, "אֶהְיֶה עִמָּךְ *Ehyeh imakh*—I will be with you" (Exodus 3:11–12).

What kind of answer is this? Moses is looking for reassurance that he is the man for the job. God's response is simply to say, "I will be with you," as if to say, "Moses, when you feel most hopeless and alone, you are not alone. Know that I am with you."

In response to Moses's doubts, God does not promise certainty. God promises company. Moses will overcome his despair and once more find his voice because he remembers that he is not alone.

Psalm 23 declares, "Though I walk through the valley of the shadow of death, I will fear no evil, for You are with me." I take this verse to heart whenever I find myself accompanying someone on a journey of grief or despair. I cannot walk that lonesome valley for you, but I can keep you company along the way. Perhaps my presence can remind you of a greater Presence that is also urging you forward. When you feel most alone, I will be with you.

At the end of every synagogue service, we sing the 11th-century hymn *Adon Olam.* I sang it countless times growing up, but never stopped to consider its meaning, other than that it meant the service was finally over. But now I know why we walk out of the synagogue with that song on our lips, for it closes with this couplet: "Into your hands I entrust my spirit, while I sleep and when I wake, and as long as my breath is in my body, God is with me, and I will not fear."

The Divine promise to Moses is also given to us.

By fortunate happenstance, the weekly portions that tell of the exodus from Egypt fall in January and coincide with the national commemoration of the Rev. Dr. Martin Luther King Jr.'s birthday. In my congregation, we always make the connection between our ancient story of liberation from bondage with the modern struggle for African-American liberation, and Dr. King's transformational leadership in that effort. In that spirit, I want to quote Dr. King as he described a harrowing moment when he, like Moses in our narrative, felt most alone and was considering giving up his struggle. Sitting at his kitchen table with his head in his hands, King writes:

> At that moment I experienced the presence of the Divine ... I could hear the quiet assurance of an inner voice, saying, "Stand up for righteousness, stand up for truth. God will be at your side forever." Almost at once my fears began to pass from me. My uncertainty disappeared. I was ready to face anything. The outer situation remained the same, but God had given me inner calm.[2]

In our darkest moments, may we all sense the presence of the power of life accompanying us, supporting us and reminding us that we are not alone.

---

2. Martin Luther King, Jr., from a sermon, "Our God Is Able," delivered in 1956 during the Montgomery bus boycott. It appears in print in *Strength to Love* (Philadelphia: Fortress Press, 1963), p.114.

15 —————————————————————————

Bo | בא

Martin Luther King Is My Rabbi

וַיָּבֹא מֹשֶׁה וְאַהֲרֹן אֶל־פַּרְעֹה וַיֹּאמְרוּ אֵלָיו כֹּה־אָמַר יְהֹוָה
אֱלֹהֵי הָעִבְרִים עַד־מָתַי מֵאַנְתָּ לֵעָנֹת מִפָּנָי שַׁלַּח עַמִּי וְיַעַבְדֻנִי:

*Va'yavo Moshe v'Aharon el Par'oh va'yomru eilav, "Ko
amar YHVH, Elohei ha'Ivrim: Ad matai mei'anta
lei'anot mipanai? Shalakh ami vaya'avduni!"*

So Moses and Aaron went to Pharaoh and said to him, "Thus
says the Source of Life, the God of the Hebrews: How long will
you refuse to humble yourself before me? Let my people go,
that they may serve the Source of Life!" (Exodus 10:3).

OUR TORAH TELLS AN ageless and inspiring story. Every year when our
cycle of readings brings us to the telling of the Exodus from slavery, I am
stirred once again by the central message of our people's journey: We affirm that there is a Power inherent in the fabric of the universe that insists
that human beings be free from subjugation and tyranny—that all people
bear the imprint of Divinity, and therefore must be treated with dignity
and respect. We know that any of us, in our lust for power, can willfully
ignore this moral law, harden our hearts and become like Pharaoh. In our

selfishness, we can spurn the demands of justice and instead focus solely on personal gain.

This was as true in ancient Israel as it is today. After the Children of Israel conquered the land of Canaan and established their own kingdoms of Judah and Israel, they forgot the covenant they had long ago sworn to uphold at Mount Sinai. In that milieu, a series of prophets arose: spokespeople for the God of Sinai. The prophets railed against the injustices, oppression and complacency that overtook Israelite society, and reminded high and low alike that their God would not be satisfied with rote worship and meaningless proclamations. The prophets' words became canonized, their elevated rhetoric forever amplifying the teaching of the Exodus: Our task as human beings is to be neither tyrant nor slave, but rather servants of YHVH, Life Unfolding. This is the fundamental message of Judaism. As Jews we are called upon to serve, bear witness to, and align ourselves with the God of Justice and Freedom.

This truth can become buried, however, in the struggle for survival. In the face of all the Pharaohs throughout history who have tried to hurl our babies into the Nile, to this very day we Jews can close ranks and read the story of the Exodus as merely a promise of our own survival, rather than as the bearer of soaring truths about the human condition. In the rote repetition of the tale, we also run the risk of becoming inured to its deeper message. How do we awaken again to the universal message of our story?

The African-American struggle for freedom and equality showed me the way. The Africans who were captured from their homes and forced into slavery in the New World were also forced to adopt their masters' religion. But subversively, as these African slaves listened to their masters' Bible, they heard their own lives in the story of the slaves in Egypt. The seeds of their own hope and liberation were embedded in the very heart of the teaching that their oppressors had forced upon them. When they sang "When Israel was in Egypt land . . . Let My people go," they made the ancient story vibrate with new life and urgency.

Again, in this *parashah*, I turn to the Rev. Dr. Martin Luther King Jr., who fully understood the inspiring power of the story of the Exodus and the hope it gave to African-Americans. He embraced the prophetic voice of justice that is at the heart of the Hebrew Bible, and he awakened me to the inspiring message of my own heritage.

Dr. King's "I Have a Dream" speech, delivered from the steps of the Lincoln Memorial on Aug. 28, 1963, is replete with biblical references:

Now is the time to make justice a reality for all of God's children
... [And] we will not be satisfied until justice rolls down like water
and righteousness like a mighty stream ...

Dr. King is quoting the Prophet Amos, who spoke these words in the
name of God to the community of Israel in the eighth century BCE:

Spare me the sound of your hymns and the music of your lutes.
Rather, let justice roll down like waters, and righteousness
like a mighty stream! (Amos 5:21–25).

Then Dr. King quotes the Prophet Isaiah (Isaiah 40:3–5):

I have a dream that one day "every valley shall be exalted, and
every hill and mountain shall be made low; the rough places will
be made plain, and the crooked places will be made straight; and
the glory of the Lord shall be revealed, and all flesh shall see it
together."

Dr. King frequently invoked the journey of Moses and the Children
of Israel towards the Promised Land as the template for his own people's
struggle. He recognized it as a journey we need to take in each and every
generation. On April 3, 1968, the night before he was murdered, Dr. King
compared his own story to that of Moses and etched this indelible image
with his final words:

Well, I don't know what will happen now. We've got some difficult
days ahead. But it doesn't matter with me now. Because I've been
to the mountaintop. And I don't mind. Like anybody, I would like
to live a long life. Longevity has its place. But I'm not concerned
about that now. I just want to do God's will. And He's allowed me
to go up to the mountain. And I've looked over. And I've seen the
promised land. I may not get there with you. But I want you to
know tonight, that we, as a people will get to the promised land.
And I'm happy, tonight. I'm not worried about anything. I'm not
fearing any man. Mine eyes have seen the glory of the coming of
the Lord. ("I've Been to the Mountaintop" speech, 1968.)

I thank Dr. King and all African-Americans who continue to struggle
against the ingrained racism of American history and life. I thank them for
inspiring me with their fortitude and continued determination against the
external, and also the internal, warping effects of oppression. And I equally
thank them for taking my ancient story and reminding me that it speaks
to us today and every day. For this is the plain instruction of the Passover

Haggadah: "In every generation, every person must view himself or herself as personally leaving slavery in Egypt. And anyone who elaborates upon this story is to be praised!"

I thank Dr. King for bearing witness to the God or Power or Idea that I worship as a Jew and as a human being of conscience:

> ... there is something unfolding in the universe, whether one speaks of it as an unconscious process, or whether one speaks of it as unmoved mover, or whether someone speaks of it as a personal God. There is something in the universe that unfolds for justice, and so in Montgomery we felt somehow that as we struggled, we had cosmic companionship. And this was one of the things that kept the people together, the belief that the universe is on the side of justice ("The Power of Nonviolence," 1958).

"The universe is on the side of justice." By recasting religious language into modern, non-personal metaphors, Dr. King gives me a vocabulary for speaking about my faith. For I do not believe in a supernatural and commanding God who directs the universe with His will. I do not read the story of the Exodus as a historical event. I do not wonder about the historicity of the plague of frogs or the slaying of the firstborn. Yet I do have an abiding faith in this central message of the Torah: that the universe is on the side of justice, and that we should be on the side of justice as well. This is what it means to me to serve God.

May the memory of the Rev. Dr. Martin Luther King Jr. continue to inspire us, today and for generations to come.

16 ———————

Beshalakh | בשלח

Spiritual Boot Camp

וַיִּלּ֜וֹנוּ כָּל־עֲדַ֧ת בְּנֵֽי־יִשְׂרָאֵ֛ל עַל־מֹשֶׁ֥ה וְעַֽל־אַהֲרֹ֖ן בַּמִּדְבָּֽר:

Va'yilonu kol adat B'nei Yisrael al Moshe v'al Aharon bamidbar.

In the wilderness, the whole Israelite community grumbled against Moses and Aaron (Exodus 16:2).

BESHALAKH IS A MOMENTOUS Torah portion. Pharaoh, his kingdom in ruins, has finally let the Children of Israel go. They arrive at the shores of the sea, יַם סוּף *Yam Suf* (sometimes translated as Red Sea and sometimes as Sea of Reeds). Pharaoh's army pursues them. God commands Moses to hold his staff out over the waters, and a strong wind blows all night, parting the waters. The Children of Israel "walked on dry ground through the sea, the waters forming a wall on their right and on their left" (Exodus 14:22). Pharaoh's chariots' wheels bog down; water crashes over them. "Pharaoh's army got drownded," as the famous spiritual goes.

Moses and Miriam and the Children of Israel sing and rejoice and celebrate. They have been liberated from Pharaoh's bondage. They are free! Now what?

Grumbling. Complaining. The Hebrew word is וַיִּלֹּנוּ *va'yilonu*:

> The people grumbled against Moses: "What shall we drink" (Exodus 15:24)?

> The whole community grumbled against Moses and Aaron: "We wish YHVH had killed us in the land of Egypt, when we sat by the pots of meat and ate our fill of bread. You brought us out to this wilderness to starve!" (Exodus 16:3).

> The people grumbled against Moses: "Why did you bring us up from Egypt—to kill us and our children and livestock from thirst?" (Exodus 17:3).

Chapter after chapter of complaining. Finally, Moses cries to God (and this is an actual translation):

> What am I supposed to do with these people? Before long they will be stoning me!" (Exodus 17:4).

This story always reminds me of my brothers and me fighting and complaining in the back of the station wagon on long car trips. I'm sure my parents felt similarly to Moses, wondering why they had ever thought that taking us on a trip was a good idea! Perhaps that is why in Hebrew the Israelites are called בְּנֵי יִשְׂרָאֵל *B'nei Yisrael*, the Children of Israel. In Egypt, they possessed no autonomy. Now that they are free, they face the daunting tasks of autonomy: They must learn to delay gratification, take responsibility for themselves, build a just and fair society, and have faith in their future. These are the prerequisites for self-determination. If they do not master these attributes, then even if physically they are no longer enslaved, emotionally and spiritually they will never be ready to enter their land of promise, their Promised Land. This maturation process will take 40 years.

For each complaint in our Torah portion, God provides a solution: Brackish waters are made sweet; quail and manna cover the ground with food; Moses strikes a rock with his powerful staff, and water gushes from stone.

But these are not merely miraculous fixes. The Torah also describes them as tests for the Children of Israel. YHVH is training them so that they might be able to endure the insecurity of freedom and still rise each day with faith in the journey.

The deepest exposition of the nature of this training is Chapter 16 of Exodus. The entire chapter is devoted to the story of the manna, the fine and flaky substance that appears on the ground every morning to feed the entire community. Manna is no ordinary food. When the Children of Israel went out to gather it, whether they gathered much or little, each household discovered that it had exactly the quantity they needed to be satiated. If anyone tried to hoard the manna and save the excess, the next morning they would find that the manna had rotted and was now putrid. On the day before Shabbat, everyone was instructed to collect a double portion so that they would not have to labor on Shabbat; lo and behold, on Shabbat, the manna did not turn foul. What is this wondrous food?

That is precisely the question that the Children of Israel asked when they first saw the flakes covering the ground like frost: "מָן הוּא? *Mahn hu?*—What is it?" (Exodus 16:15). And thus, they named it *Mahn;* in English, manna. The name manna means "What is it?" There was no suitable name for this nourishment from God—only a daily, amazed exclamation at the sustenance being provided to them. As our morning prayers declare, "with goodness and compassion you renew every day Creation's wondrous work."

This was the "spiritual boot camp" of the Israelites' sojourn in the wilderness. Every day, they had to practice faith that with each new day, they would receive that which they needed. Their impulse to hoard was stymied and useless. Day by day, they were challenged to overcome their fear of not having enough and instead trust in Life Unfolding.

I view the wilderness sojourn metaphorically. As I rise to enter a new day, my default attitude is self-interest—making sure I'm going to get my share today. But that attitude thrusts me forward, aggressively, into my experience. What if I instead started my day saying, "Thank you"? What if I relaxed my grip on life and trusted enough to let it come to me? Even more prosaically, what if while I stand in a line of hungry people at a potluck, I could assume that I am not going to starve, and instead breathe deeply and wish everyone well? What if I had more faith, more wonder and more gratitude? Might that be the training I need to enter my Promised Land? Might I find that I am, in fact, already dwelling in my Promised Land at the moments when I stop grasping and instead start gasping in wonder at the countless ways I am already provided for? At those moments, I forget to grumble and complain. At those moments, I naturally only take what I need and happily share the rest. Day by day, I am learning the lesson of the manna.

17 ——————————————————

Yitro | יתרו

The Ten Utterances

אָנֹכִי יְהֹוָה אֱלֹהֶיךָ אֲשֶׁר הוֹצֵאתִיךָ מֵאֶרֶץ מִצְרַיִם מִבֵּית עֲבָדִים:

Anokhi YHVH Elohekha asher hotzeitikha mei'eretz Mitzrayim mi'beit avadim.

I am Life Unfolding who brought you out of constriction and enslavement (Exodus 20:2).

AFTER WEEKS OF JOURNEYING from the Red Sea, the Children of Israel arrive at the foot of Mount Sinai. There, after careful preparations, they hear the voice of God and receive what are known in English as the Ten Commandments. The Hebrew term, however, is not עֲשֶׂרֶת הַמִצְוֹת *Aseret Hamitzvot—mitzvot* meaning "commandments." In Jewish tradition, the words at Mount Sinai are known as עֲשֶׂרֶת הַדִּבְּרוֹת *Aseret Hadibrot*, "The Ten Utterances."

In all of the Torah, this is the only time when the entire People are addressed directly by God, rather than through God's messenger, Moses. Therefore, the "Utterances" are elevated to a special status. The rabbis are fascinated by this unique occurrence and weave rich images to describe the mystery of an entire people simultaneously hearing God's voice.

For what does it mean to hear God speak? Did the multitudes around the mountain all hear the same amplified announcement, like a giant public address system at a ballpark? Our sages find this kind of literal rendering absurd; the voice of God, a message emanating from the Infinite Source of Life, is of a different order than a human voice. "God's voice" must be understood metaphorically. If God is infinite, from where does God's voice emanate? Do we hear God's voice with our ears or with our hearts? Is God's voice even in human language, or is it perhaps a pre-verbal revelation that we then struggle to approximate within the limitations of the spoken word?

The Torah itself challenges any literal understanding of how one might hear God's voice. In the book of Kings, Elijah the prophet—second only to Moses in stature as a prophet who communicates directly with God—also travels to the Holy Mountain to hear God's voice. In our portion, the mountain quakes and smokes, and thunder resounds, so overwhelming is the voice of God. But in Elijah's encounter, he hears God not in the thunder or the raging wind or quaking earth, but rather in a קוֹל דְּמָמָה דַקָּה *kol d'mamah dakah*, usually translated as a "still, small voice," but even better rendered as "the fine sound of silence." Elijah hears God in the sound of silence. It appears that the passage about Elijah is offering a pointed contrast to the bombast and pyrotechnics of *Yitro*: God's voice sometimes might overpower us like an earthquake, but at other times requires of us profound stillness in order to be discerned.

The sages build on this paradox at length by suggesting that perhaps God doesn't have anything at all comparable to a human voice—that all visions and versions of God are and can only be human interpretations of a reality so sublime that it cannot be captured in any single description. For example, the third-century sage Rabbi Yochanan points to the first word of the Ten Utterances, אָנֹכִי *Anokhi*—"I am"—and suggests that for the Israelites, coming into the unmediated presence of the Infinite was more than they could handle. What each one of them did finally hear was filtered through their own being, and therefore, was never exactly the same as their neighbor:

> Rabbi Yochanan taught: The moment Israel at Sinai heard the *Anokhi* their souls left them, and they died! Therefore, God revived them and thereafter spoke to each person according to their own capacity. Furthermore, all at Mount Sinai, young and old, men, women, children and infants, received God's word according to their ability to understand. Even Moses understood only according to his capacity (Shemot Rabbah 5:9).

The followers of Rabbi Ishmael put it this way:

> The School of Rabbi Ishmael taught: Just as a hammer that strikes a rock causes sparks to fly off in all directions, so each and every word that issued from the mouth of the Holy One divided itself into seventy languages. (Babylonian Talmud, Tractate Shabbat 88b)

Traditionally, 70 represents the totality of human languages. The "word" of God refracts endlessly through every tongue and according to each person's unique ability to understand. The Ten Utterances in our received Torah text are understood simultaneously to be authoritative and in need of interpretation. I trust this paradoxical approach because for me it is hubris for a person ever to claim full understanding, even as we affirm that Truth exists. Every written or spoken word of Torah (even the Ten Utterances) is and can only be a draft, awaiting our further refinement as we work on refining ourselves. Jewish tradition understands Mount Sinai more as a state of consciousness than as a specific historical event or location. We assert that anyone who encounters God's voice reverberating in their being is "standing at Mount Sinai."

Recently, I tried an experiment. I spent time contemplating the Ten Utterances, and reflected on my years of study and reflection. Emptying myself as best as I could, I allowed myself to write my current draft of my understanding of these ancient words. I share them with you here, and hope that as you read them, they strike more sparks in the ongoing revelation of God's voice. Perhaps I got to join the crowd at the foot of Mount Sinai. It certainly felt that way.

The Ten Utterances from Life Unfolding

1. I am Life Unfolding who brought you out of constriction and enslavement so that you might serve me and be in relationship to me. No one said this was going to be easy.

2. Place no gods of your own making in between you and Life Unfolding. Do not make an image or a fixed concept of Life Unfolding and attempt to serve only that fixed concept. Life Unfolding is infinite and ever-expanding, and cannot be reduced to a static idea.

3. You are as good as your word. Beware: If you invoke Life Unfolding as a witness to the truth of your words, you will be held to account for them. Do not overestimate your own power to speak and fulfill.

4. Make one day out of seven holy, a Sabbath, in which you relinquish illusions of control over Creation. Remember on this day that you are creature, not creator. Humbly and joyfully take your place in the chorus of Creation. On this day, you may not lord it over any person or creature under your temporary authority. Rather, stand side by side with them in gratitude for Life Unfolding.

5. Honor your parents, for however imperfectly they fulfilled their task, they have been the vessels and agents of My purpose, which was to bring you into the world as a new expression of Life Unfolding.

6. Do not murder, for every human life is a reflection of infinite possibility, and when you destroy a life you destroy a part of Me, Life Unfolding.

7. Do not commit adultery, for a marriage is a sacred covenant and you gave your word. If you are to realize your potential as an agent and partner of Life Unfolding, you must strive to be as good as your word. No one said this was going to be easy.

8. Do not steal. Treat everyone and everything with fundamental respect.

9. Do not bear false witness against others. When you speak of them, remember that they are children of Life Unfolding and nothing less. Witness them in this light, so that your words may be compassionate and true. Choose your words with great care; they have the power to create and to destroy.

10. Do not covet. Rather, practice radical gratitude at all times for the gift of Life Unfolding, of which you are the beneficiary. This is the key to true liberation. No one said this was going to be easy.

18 ————————————————————

Mishpatim | משפטים

YHVH, Protector of the Powerless

כָּל־אַלְמָנָה וְיָתוֹם לֹא תְעַנּוּן: אִם־עַנֵּה תְעַנֶּה אֹתוֹ כִּי אִם־צָעֹק
יִצְעַק אֵלַי שָׁמֹעַ אֶשְׁמַע צַעֲקָתוֹ:

*Kol almanah v'yatom lo t'anun. Im aneih t'aneh oto ki
im tza'ok yitz'ak eilai shamo'a esh'ma tza'akato.*

You are not to mistreat any widow or orphan. Oh, if you
mistreat, mistreat them, and they cry, cry out to Me, I will
hearken, yes, hearken to their outcry (Exodus 22:21–22).

IN BIBLICAL HEBREW, WHEN an emphatic statement is made, there are
no words such as "surely" or "really," and certainly no boldface or italics
or exclamation points available. Instead, the verb is repeated twice. In the
verse above, we know that the Hebrew is being unusually forceful because
not one, but every verb in the verse is repeated twice. Most English translations do not reflect this feature of biblical Hebrew and instead aim for a
more literary English rendering. Unfortunately, the reader of those translations misses the thrust of the Hebrew. When we read the Hebrew, we need

to imagine this verse as a bold headline, in giant letters, shouting at us from the page: "Pay Attention to This Instruction!"[1]

And of what are we being asked to take special notice? That YHVH hears the cry of the widow and orphan. YHVH hears the cry of the powerless and will protect them. This theme is emphatically repeated many times in the Torah. For example:

> If you take, take your neighbor's garment as a security against a debt, you must return it before the sun sets. It is his only available covering—in what else shall he sleep? If that person cries out to Me, I will hearken, for I am compassionate (Exodus 22:25–26).

> If there is a needy person among you . . . do not harden your heart and shut your hand against them. Rather, open, open your hand; lend, lend what is sufficient to meet their need, their need . . . If you do not give and they cry out to YHVH, you will incur guilt. Give, give with a full heart in your giving, and YHVH will bless you in all your efforts (Deuteronomy 15:7–10).

In the patriarchal social structure of ancient Israel (which still exists today in many parts of the world), every person who belonged to a clan had a גּוֹאֵל go'eil—a redeemer, or protector, who was the leader of that clan or family. If someone fell into captivity, the go'eil was responsible to redeem them from enslavement. If someone fell into poverty, the go'eil was responsible for their sustenance. But there were some who had no go'eil: the widow, the orphan and the stranger. If misfortune befell them, they had no one to count on to bail them out or to rescue them. In fact, they had no legal recourse at all; they were truly the powerless in that society.

The Torah lays out a legal and communal imperative to transcend what it sees as an inherent flaw of that societal structure. The Torah seeks to make everyone, including those who have no protector, as fully meriting fair and equal protection under the law. This is a radical and unprecedented ideal that our Torah offered to the ancient world, and it should not be overlooked by the modern reader.

But how does a society enforce a new norm that falls outside of any existing precedent? We must remember that there is no apparent incentive for individuals to embrace this principle. The powerless by definition have nothing to offer in return for their protection. They don't even have

---

1. See *The Five Books of Moses: A New Translation* by Everett Fox for his unusual rendering that preserves the cadences of the biblical Hebrew.

a protector who can exact revenge against your clan if you mistreat them. There is no obvious self-interest in caring for these unfortunates.

Therefore, Judaism makes an audacious claim—a claim that resonates in our moral codes to this day: YHVH, the Creator of the Universe and of all human beings, is the protector of the powerless. They are, as it were, in their Creator's clan, even if they are unfortunate enough to have no human *goʾeil*. Furthermore, the Torah makes clear that we Jews were the test case to show the world that the Creator indeed sides with the weak against those that would mistreat them. For we were slaves in Egypt, and our situation was hopeless by any existing standard for we had no redeemer. But God heard our cry and redeemed us from bondage:

> And YHVH said, "I have seen, yes, I have seen the mistreatment of
> My people in Mitzrayim, and I have heard their outcry on account
> of their oppressors; yes, I know their pain" (Exodus 3:7).

In order to enshrine this new imperative that asserts that it is our responsibility to protect the weak and powerless even if they are not our close kin, our tradition insists that the God we worship is the model that we must follow. Furthermore, if we do not embody this imperative, the Torah asserts that YHVH is watching, and as the *goʾeil* of the weak, YHVH will bestow blessing if we walk in God's ways, though will exact retribution if we do not. We are meant to behave the way our Creator behaves and extend ourselves to those who cannot fend for themselves.

And if the promise of Divine retribution and reward is not sufficient, the Torah employs another method of incentive to motivate us to treat as equals those who bring us no obvious benefit: again, and again, it calls on us to empathize. Our Torah portion declares,

> You shall not oppress a stranger, for you know the feelings of the
> stranger, having yourselves been strangers in the land of Egypt
> (Exodus 23:9).

And elsewhere in the Torah:

> When you reap the harvest of your field and overlook a sheaf, do
> not turn back to get it; it shall go to the stranger, the orphan and
> the widow ... When you gather the grapes of your vineyard, do
> not pick it over again; that shall go to the stranger, the orphan and
> the widow. Always remember that you were a slave in the land of
> Egypt (Deuteronomy 24:19–22).

Or:

> When an indentured servant goes free after his six years of service, do not let him go empty-handed. Furnish him out of the flock, threshing floor, and vat with which YHVH your God has blessed you. Remember that you were a slave in the land of Egypt and that YHVH your God redeemed you (Deuteronomy 14:12–15).

Our prayer book declares: מָה יָפֶה יְרֻשָּׁתֵנוּ *Mah yafeh yerushateinu!*—"How beautiful is our heritage!" This phrase comes to my lips as I reflect on the world-changing message of empathy and justice in our Torah, proclaimed as emphatically as biblical Hebrew knows how and kept alive through every generation since so that it reaches our ears, our minds and our hearts: Caring for your kin is a self-evident virtue. Looking out for your neighbor is common sense; you scratch their back, and they will scratch yours. But our tradition insists that beyond these circles of obvious concern and self-interest, even the powerless merit our care and our energy for they, too, are God's children, and they, the same as any of us, deserve to be redeemed.

19

Terumah | תרומה

Creating Holy Moments

דַּבֵּר אֶל־בְּנֵי יִשְׂרָאֵל וְיִקְחוּ־לִי תְּרוּמָה מֵאֵת כָּל־אִישׁ אֲשֶׁר
יִדְּבֶנּוּ לִבּוֹ תִּקְחוּ אֶת־תְּרוּמָתִי: . . . וְעָשׂוּ לִי מִקְדָּשׁ וְשָׁכַנְתִּי
בְּתוֹכָם:

*Dabeir el B'nei Yisrael v'yikkhu li terumah mei'eit kol
ish asher yidvenu libo tik'khu et trumati . . . V'asu li
mikdash v'shakhanti b'tocham.*

Tell the Children of Israel to bring Me gifts—you shall accept
gifts for Me from every person whose heart so moves them . . .
And you shall build Me a sanctuary and I will dwell in your
midst (Exodus 25:2, 8).

PRIOR TO REVEALING THE Ten Commandments and their accompanying ordinances, God explained that if the Children of Israel fulfilled these
mitzvot (commandments) they would become a גּוֹי קָדוֹשׁ *goy kadosh*—a
"holy people" (Exodus 19:6).

The word קָדוֹשׁ *kadosh*—"holy" or "sacred"—is a central term in Jewish life, and even if you do not know any Hebrew, you are probably familiar
with its variants: we recite קַדִּישׁ *Kaddish* in memory of the dead, we recite

קִדּוּש *Kiddush* over the Shabbat wine, and the ancient Temple in Jerusalem was the בֵּית הַמִּקְדָּש *Beit Hamikdash*, the "House of Holiness"—all variants on the root meaning "holy." Clearly, our assignment as Jews is to manifest קְדֻשָׁה *kedushah* ("holiness") in the world.

In the language of the Torah, *kedushah* is a place or moment in which we experience the presence of the Divine. Judaism is acutely aware of the paradox inherent in this formulation. Is not the entire world already suffused with Divine Presence? And yet, we humans are uniquely capable of being oblivious to this sublime truth. We can be so self-centered that we treat others as objects for our self-gratification, and we treat the world as our possession to exploit. We desecrate God's creation. Jewish tradition unequivocally claims that holiness pervades every particle of the universe. Our liturgy imagines the heavenly chorus of angels singing continuously, blissfully, proclaiming, "Holy, Holy, Holy is the Creator of All, the whole earth is filled with Divine Glory!" and invites us to join in that ecstatic affirmation. Yet we remain stubbornly capable of willful ignorance.

The Hasidic master Rabbi Menachem Mendl of Kotzk famously asked his disciples, "Tell me, where can God be found?" The students enthusiastically replied, "Why, Rebbe, everywhere, of course! Does not the Torah tell us that the whole earth is filled with Divine Glory!" "No," said the rabbi, "God can only be found where we let God in."

It is in this sense that Judaism teaches that God "needs" us. Of course, this personified language is poetic; even the earliest commentators, when speaking about God in these very human terms, would qualify their statements with the phrase כִּבְיָכוֹל *kivyakhol,* meaning "as it were." The point is, it is clear that we have a vital role to play in bringing a sense of holiness into our consciousness and our communities. Without our spiritual participation, the holiness that is incipient in every place and every moment might not be realized, might be squandered or missed. It is in that sense that God—the glory that fills and animates the universe—"needs" us to become aware of the glorious potential of every moment and interaction.

God "needs" us to create holy spaces and holy moments in which the Divine Presence can dwell. Rabbi Abraham Joshua Heschel called this state of consciousness "radical amazement." If I am able to be amazed by the person or place before me, then I have invited holiness into the world. I have made a place for God to dwell in our midst. Aware of this infinite bounty before me, how could I in that moment respond with anything but reverence, gratitude and generosity? This is a holy moment, a blessing for both the giver and the receiver (and who is actually the giver or the receiver in such moments?).

This week's *parashah, Terumah*, instructs us to build a *mikdash*, a holy space in our midst. The chapters are filled with the details of construction: the ark, the menorah, the altar, the enclosure. We can easily get lost in these details and forget their symbolic purpose as reminders of the Divine potential inherent in our shared lives.

The crucial directive we are to follow is expressed, as is often the case, in the opening instruction of the *parashah: Me'et kol ish asher yidvenu libo tik'khu et trumati*—"You shall accept gifts for Me from every person whose heart so moves them." The first prerequisite for creating a dwelling place for the Divine in our midst is that it must be freely offered. Holy interactions cannot be mandated or coerced, and the sanctuary—the dwelling place for the Divine Presence that we build in our midst—will always be the result of the offerings of our hearts. The Torah later mandates an annual fixed amount that every Israelite must give for the upkeep of the sanctuary. But the creation of this sanctuary can only take place through the outpouring of unforced generosity.

Think of a moment when you experienced a Presence greater than you could describe. There are easy moments: holding a baby, watching a sunset. And there are moments that take more cultivation: intimate love, deeds of lovingkindness. And there are moments that simply take us by surprise: a spontaneous insight, a beam of sunlight angling through a ruined landscape, an act of goodness from a stranger. Holy, holy, holy, it is our challenge and privilege to perceive these holy moments and to string them together like beads of awareness into a dwelling place for God in our lives.

V'asu li Mikdash v'shakhanti b'tokham—"And you shall build Me a sanctuary and I will dwell in your midst."

20

Tetzaveh | תצוה

Brothers' Keepers

וְעָשִׂיתָ בִגְדֵי־קֹדֶשׁ לְאַהֲרֹן אָחִיךָ לְכָבוֹד וּלְתִפְאָרֶת:

V'asita vigday kodesh l'Aharon akhikha l'khavod u'l'tifaret.

You shall make sacred garments for your brother Aaron, to give him honor and splendor (Exodus 28:2).

CURIOUSLY, THIS WEEK'S TORAH portion, *Tetzaveh*, never mentions Moses by name. This is the only Torah portion from Moses's birth at the beginning of the book of Exodus until the Children of Israel reach the far banks of the Jordan at the end of the book of Numbers in which Moses's name does not appear.

This anomaly presents a bonanza for Torah commentators like me: What deeper understandings and teachings can be derived from Moses's unusual absence? *Tetzaveh* transpires while Moses is up on Mount Sinai, receiving instructions from YHVH on how the Children of Israel are to build and maintain the מִשְׁכָּן *Mishkan*, the portable sanctuary that will be a dwelling place for the Divine Presence as the Children of Israel travel through the wilderness. In *Tetzaveh* specifically, Moses receives the instructions for how to make the sacred garments that his brother Aaron will wear as הַכֹּהֵן הַגָּדֹל *ha'Kohein ha'Gadol,* the High Priest, and how Moses is to ordain Aaron (and Aaron's sons) for this position. While YHVH is certainly addressing Moses in *Tetzaveh,* Moses is exclusively addressed as "you," never by name; the focus is entirely on Aaron, Moses's brother.

One might say that the first exchange of questions in the Torah sets the agenda for the entire teaching that we have inherited. After Cain slays his brother, Abel, because YHVH preferred Abel's offering over his own, God asks, "Where is your brother Abel?" To which Cain makes the petulant, defiant reply, "Am I my brother's keeper?" This question hovers over the remainder of the book of Genesis. Ishmael mocks his brother Isaac, and the two grow up separated. We infer that they might have reconciled when they come together to bury their father Abraham. Far from looking out for his twin brother, Esau, Jacob instead repeatedly plots to supersede him. Joseph's brothers plot to kill him because he flaunts their father's special affection for him. Only much later do they come together, and despite Joseph's forgiveness, his brothers are clearly suspicious that he harbors a grudge; as such, they live together in Egypt under Joseph's largesse in an uneasy peace. It is not a relationship of peers, but Joseph does answer the question "Am I my brothers' keeper?" with an unequivocal yes. This is where the book of Genesis ends.

Exodus introduces us to the next set of brothers; Moses and Aaron demonstrate a heretofore unseen and inspirational level of "brother-keeping." The brothers are very different from each other and have different strengths as leaders. But rather than compete for the top role, they collaborate, largely without one-upmanship. Their relationship is presented as one of loving respect. At the burning bush, Moses once again demurs from God's call to him to go speak to Pharaoh. He claims that he can't speak well. YHVH says,

> Is there not your brother Aaron? He speaks readily. Even now he is setting out to meet you, and his heart will be glad when he sees you (Exodus 4:14).

"His heart will be glad when he sees you." How different this is from the meetings of brothers in Genesis:

> When the messengers came back to Jacob, they said, "Your brother Esau is coming to meet you, accompanied by four hundred men." And Jacob was terrified . . . (Genesis 32:7–8).

Or:

> "I am your brother Joseph—Is my father really alive?" But his brothers were unable to answer him—they recoiled in fear of him (Genesis 45:3).

Rabbi Jonathan Sacks comments:

> The brothers [Moses and Aaron] work together from the very outset of the mission to lead the Israelites to freedom. They address the people together. They stand together when confronting Pharaoh. They perform signs and wonders together. They share leadership of the people in the wilderness together. For the first time, brothers function as a team, with different gifts, different talents, different roles, but without hostility, each complementing the other.[1]

Rabbi Sacks is following an ancient *midrashic* line. When Aaron goes out to meet Moses, the Torah relates "And he kissed him" (Exodus 4:27). The *midrash* comments: This means: Each rejoiced at the other's greatness (Shemot Rabbah 5:10).

Of course, over the next 40 years, Moses and Aaron have disagreements and conflicts. They are human. Aaron even challenges Moses's leadership at one point. But the fundamental humility exhibited by Moses always transcends the difficulty. He truly does not think of himself in any way as someone exceptionally entitled or special. Despite being the younger brother, Moses never tries to usurp his brother's role. Again, what a contrast to Jacob or Joseph!

So, why does Moses's name not appear in our *parashah*? Because in all of these instructions dedicated to investing Aaron in his leadership role, Moses feels no need to interject himself. In fact, he wants to get out of the way, when the spotlight is meant to be on his brother. This is reflected in our verse, "You shall make sacred garments for your brother Aaron, to give him honor and splendor" (Exodus 28:2). Just as Aaron was happy in his heart to see Moses, so Moses is truly happy to give his brother honor and splendor, equal to his own.

As the *midrash* phrases it so eloquently, "each rejoiced at the other's greatness." In this week's *parashah*, it is Aaron's turn to shine, and Moses cedes center stage with grace. Neither needed to overshadow the other's light in order to feel fulfilled. May we all learn from their example.

1. *www.rabbisacks.org/covenant-conversation-5770-tetzaveh-who-is-honoured/*

21 ———————————————————

Ki Tisa | כי תשא

Encountering God

וְעַתָּה אִם־נָא מָצָאתִי חֵן בְּעֵינֶיךָ הוֹדִעֵנִי נָא אֶת־דְּרָכֶךָ וְאֵדָעֲךָ

V'atah, im na matzati hein b'einekha, hodi'eni na et d'rakhekha, v'eida'akha

[Moses said,] "And now, please, if I have found favor in your eyes, please let me know your ways, that I may know you" (Exodus 33:13).

וַיֹּאמַר הַרְאֵנִי נָא אֶת־כְּבֹדֶךָ:

Vayomar "Har'eini na et k'vodekha!"

And [Moses] said, "Please, let me behold Your Presence!" (Exodus 33:18).

HOW DOES THE TORAH describe God? Not by doctrine or dogma, but by encounter. Not with systematic theology, but with stories. I find this approach refreshing. Stories do not demand agreement or adherence; they invite engagement. We hear a story, and we live that story, imagining it, putting ourselves into the scene. "Once upon a time" is, in fact, always "now," as time collapses and we immerse ourselves in the narrative. Stories also can never be reduced to one meaning; they demand interpretation, and we humans delight in plumbing what a good story might mean.

A theology or a creed attempts to fix a particular conception of the nature of our infinite reality, which in religious shorthand we refer to in English as "God." This approach, while certainly of value, will always fall short of a full apprehension of reality because the infinite cannot be defined. It is oxymoronic to try to define that which is infinite, that which has no limit. On the other hand, while we cannot define that which is infinite, we can certainly encounter and have a relationship with the infinite reality that we perceive around and within us. When we pause and gaze at a starry sky, we encounter the infinite mystery. When we pause and look into another human face, we encounter that which we can never fully understand. And yet, we yearn to know more deeply, to encounter more intimately.

We can have a relationship with that which is beyond our complete understanding: YHVH, Life Unfolding. The Torah tells us stories about our ancestors' encounters with that mystery and bequeaths to us not a fixed definition of God, which cannot be contained in any final description, but a call to encounter God. This takes courage. The Infinite not only fascinates, draws us and compels us. It's also terrifying! At Mount Sinai, after the revelation, the people trembled and fell back from the mountain.

> You speak to us," they said to Moses, "and we will listen, but let not God speak with us any further, lest we die!" Moses said, "Be not afraid!" . . . But the people remained at a distance, while Moses approached the thick cloud where God was (Exodus 21:15–18).

Moses is our hero, the one who somehow is willing and able to walk into that thick cloud of unknowing and encounter the Infinite:

> וַיְדַבֵּר יְהֹוָה אֶל־מֹשֶׁה פָּנִים אֶל־פָּנִים כַּאֲשֶׁר יְדַבֵּר אִישׁ אֶל־רֵעֵהוּ

> *Vdiber YHVH el Moshe panim el panim, ka'asher ydabeir ish el rei'eihu*—"YHVH would speak to Moses face to face, as one person speaks to another" (Exodus 33:11).

Moses is fearless, engaging the Great Mystery in impassioned discourse, arguing for the life of his people despite their terrors and smallness and cowardice, and despite their unwillingness to engage in the relationship that YHVH desires to have with them, to have with each of us.

As I read the Torah, along with countless commentators before me, I come to this conclusion: God, the Infinite Mystery of our being, desires us (to use human terminology, which is all we've got) and longs to know us face to face. In this week's portion, the Children of Israel reject that relationship in favor of the Golden Calf. Most of the time we are like the Children of Israel; on occasion, we stumble out of our daily preoccupations and catch a glimpse of the awesome and endless wonder that surrounds us. We might sense a call from the universe—a conviction that despite our smallness, our lives matter, and that we have a place to fill and a task to perform. But awe can quickly turn to discomfort or embarrassment, even fear, as when we gaze into someone's eyes for too many beats. We retreat from the encounter, unable to sustain our gaze. Instead, we make our own Golden Calves and bow before them. We shrink our world into manageable forms (our tradition calls them "false gods") and refuse to listen to the whisper that calls to our souls. Moses is our prophet because he does not shrink away. Moses's longing to know God is so unquenchable that he ascends the mountain once again. YHVH then reveals as much of the Divine character as any human being can apprehend:

> And [Moses] said, "Please, let me behold Your Presence!" And [YHVH] answered, "I will make all My goodness pass before you, and I will display My Essence, and reveal all the grace and compassion that make up My Essence (Exodus 33:18–19).

When Moses descends from the mountain soon thereafter, carrying with him the second set of tablets, symbolic of the restored relationship with YHVH, he is transformed. His face is radiant. Light pours from his countenance, so much so that the Children of Israel initially shrink from him as they had shrunk away from the holy mountain. But then they draw near so that Moses can teach them.

Moses is our hero and our teacher because of his faith, which literally means trust. He trusts enough to walk through the terror of encountering the Infinite. He trusts enough to walk directly into the thick cloud of unknowing, the place where our intense desire to define and control reality is nullified. He trusts enough to become intimate with that great Mystery before which we are, strangely, simultaneously, infinitesimally insignificant and also of singular importance. Moses is not able to define God—no one is—but Moses encounters God, and then brings back to us the fruits of that living relationship.

22

Vayak'hel | ויקהל

When Enough Is Enough

וְהַמְּלָאכָה הָיְתָה דַיָּם לְכָל־הַמְּלָאכָה לַעֲשׂוֹת אֹתָהּ וְהוֹתֵר:

*V'ha'melakhah hai'tah day'am l'chol ha'melakhah
la'asot otah v'hoteir.*

And their efforts had been more than enough for all the tasks
to be done (Exodus 36:7).

MOSES HAS DESCENDED ONCE again from the mountain, face aglow,
carrying the tablets with the restored covenant in his arms. God has for-
given the Children of Israel for their transgressions with the Golden Calf.
They are finally ready to begin creating God's dwelling place in the heart of
their community. Moses asks the Children of Israel to now donate and craft
all of the elements that God has instructed them to make, and they respond
with an overflowing outpouring of gifts, so much so that an unprecedented
decree is announced:

> All the artisans who were engaged in the crafting of the holy
> sanctuary, every single one of them, stopped their labors and said
> to Moses, "The people are bringing more than is needed for the
> work that God has instructed us to do!" Moses thereupon had this

proclamation made throughout the camp: "Let no man or woman make further effort towards gifts for the sanctuary!" So the people stopped bringing. Their efforts had been more than enough for all the work to be done (Exodus 36:4–7).

The Children of Israel were finally able and ready to allow their creativity and love for God to flow without stint. Yet it appears that sometimes, even expressions of love and generosity need to be curbed. When is our overflowing love too much?

Maybe this is a question I particularly face as a parent. My love for my daughters truly knows no bounds. Yet so much of the time, I find that the most loving action I can offer them is to restrain myself, and let them live their own lives and figure things out for themselves.

Our sages understand this paradox and describe the need for restraint as inherent in the very integrity of Creation. As they reflect on the creation story that begins our Torah, they note that had God's unbounded creative energy poured out unchecked, the boundaries and distinctions that make our world possible could not exist. Had God not set boundaries between the sea and the dry land, or the sky above and the waters below, the world would return to chaos. Like a painter or sculptor, God needed to know when to put the brush or chisel down—to know when to step back, rest and enjoy the results. In fact, our magnificent creation only exists because God knew when to say דַּי *dai*—"enough."[1]

The third-century Galilean sage Resh Lakish (a compelling figure in the Talmud, Resh Lakish was a former brigand who changed his ways and became a great scholar) offers a play on one of the Divine names, אֵל שַׁדַּי *El Shaddai*, to make this point. *El Shaddai* is usually translated as "God Almighty," but the actual meaning of this ancient name is obscure. Resh Lakish sees the word *dai* ("enough") embedded in *El Shaddai,* and so he reads the name as אֵל שֶׁדַּי *El She-Dai*—"The God who knows when to say, 'Enough!' " (Babylonian Talmud, Tractate Hagigah 12a).

The later *Kabbalists* express this truth with a variety of evocative images. In one version of the process of Creation, God's Divine Light was so overwhelming that no earthly vessel could contain it; instead, when the light poured in to any vessel, the vessel would shatter. Earlier in this

---

1. Many of us will be familiar with the Hebrew word דַּי *dai* from the Passover song *Dayenu. Dayenu* means "that would have been sufficient for us." *Ilu hotzianu mi Mitzrayim, dayenu!*—"Had God merely taken us out from slavery, that would have been sufficient for us!"

volume, in *Parashat Mikeitz*, we described the image of the shards of the broken vessels each concealing a Divine spark, and that our task is to find and recognize those sparks in our broken world. Another lesson we draw from this story is that God initially did not understand the need to say "enough" when creating the world. God had to learn how to contract and withhold enough pure energy so that it could be received at an intensity level appropriate to the vessels God wished to fill. In a modern analogue to this telling, we have understood that the physical universe truly is made up of energy in the form of atoms. Only an infinitesimal fraction of atomic energy is required to sustain our physical existence. If we split those atoms and release that energy willy-nilly, our world cannot contain that light and is destroyed.

In another description, God's attribute of unbounded love, known as חֶסֶד *Hesed,* in order to have any useful impact on the world, must be mediated through God's attribute of discipline and judgment, known as גְּבוּרָה *Gevurah* or דִין *Din.* This is another way of saying that our most effective creative and loving acts are those that are accompanied by our ability to discern when and in what measure to offer them. Our tradition teaches that even God must learn these lessons, and act as *El Shaddai,* the God who knows when to say "enough."

And so, as the Children of Israel pour themselves into creating the *Mishkan,* the holy sanctuary in their midst, they, too, must learn this lesson: Our unbounded desire to love is most effective when we pour it out with awareness and care, knowing when to let it flow and when to hold it in reserve. We learn that sometimes the most loving act we can perform is to wait, to watch and to know when enough is enough!

23 ─────────────────────────────

Pekudei | פקודי

Realizing Our True Nature

וַיֹּאמֶר מֹשֶׁה אֶל־בְּנֵי יִשְׂרָאֵל רְאוּ קָרָא יְהֹוָה בְּשֵׁם בְּצַלְאֵל בֶּן־
אוּרִי בֶן־חוּר לְמַטֵּה יְהוּדָה: וַיְמַלֵּא אֹתוֹ רוּחַ אֱלֹהִים בְּחָכְמָה
בִּתְבוּנָה וּבְדַעַת וּבְכָל־מְלָאכָה:

*Va'yomer Moshe el B'nei Yisrael: "Re'u, kara YHVH
b'sheim Betzalel, ben Uri, ben Hur, l'matei Yehudah,
va'yemaleh oto ru'akh Elohim b'khokhmah bi't'vunah
u'v'da'at u'v'khol melakhah."*

And Moses said to the Children of Israel: "See, the Creator has
singled out by name Betzalel, son of Uri, son of Hur, of the
tribe of Judah, endowing him with *ru'akh Elohim*—a Divine
spirit of wisdom, skill and knowledge in all manner of craft"
(Exodus 35:30–31).

THE FINAL ACT OF the book of Exodus is the actual construction of the
Mishkan, the dwelling place for the Divine Presence within the Israelite
community. A narrative arc is completed: As Exodus began, the Children
of Israel had been reduced to slaves. Pharaoh tried to extinguish the Divine

spark that dwells within all of us. God, as it were, was no longer dwelling in their midst. But "The Israelites groaned under their bondage and cried out . . . and God heard their cry" (Exodus 2:23), and the epic struggle for liberation was set in motion. The Divine spark could not be extinguished, and the slaves' full humanity would be restored.

Now, at the end of the book, the people contribute all of their wisdom, generosity and skill towards the creation of the מִשְׁכָּן *Mishkan*. *Mishkan* means "dwelling place." It comes from the same Hebrew root as שְׁכִינָה *Shekhinah*, which means "indwelling," and is that aspect of Divinity that we experience as being close to us. We encountered this word family also in *Parashat Terumah*, where God instructs us to "Build me a sanctuary that I might dwell (וְשָׁכַנְתִּי—*v'shakhanti*) in your midst" (Exodus 25:8). In this final act of the book of Exodus, all the components of the *Mishkan* are assembled, and the *Shekhinah*, the Divine Presence, is now able to fill this beautiful structure in the heart of the community.

An inspired craftsman named Betzalel is assigned the task of fashioning God's home.

> And Moses said to the Children of Israel: "See, the Creator has singled out by name Betzalel, son of Uri, son of Hur, of the tribe of Judah, endowing him with *ru'akh Elohim*—a Divine spirit of wisdom, skill and knowledge in all manner of craft" (Exodus 35:30-31).

Betzalel is endowed with רוּחַ אֱלֹהִים—*ru'akh Elohim*, a "Divine spirit." We first hear of *ru'akh Elohim* at the very beginning of Genesis:

> *V'ru'akh Elohim merakhefet al p'nei ha'mayim*—And the Divine Spirit hovered over the face of the waters (Genesis 1:2).

Ru'akh Elohim is God's creative energy, with which God is going to conceive, create and shape the world. Betzalel has been endowed with this same faculty.

So, who is Betzalel? Virtually every proper name in the Torah is loaded with metaphorical meaning, but none more so than Betzalel. His name is a contraction of the very essence of our humanness.

וַיִּבְרָא אֱלֹהִים אֶת־הָאָדָם בְּצַלְמוֹ בְּצֶלֶם אֱלֹהִים בָּרָא אֹתוֹ זָכָר וּנְקֵבָה בָּרָא אֹתָם:

> *Vayivra Elohim et ha'adam b'tzalmo, b'tzelem Elohim bara oto, zakhar u'nekevah bara otam*—And God created the human in the image of God, male and female God created them (Genesis 1:27).

בְּצַלְאֵל Betzalel's name is a contraction of בְּצֶלֶם אֱלֹהִים *B'tzelem Elohim*—בְּצֵל אֵל *B'tzel El*—meaning, "In the image of God." Betzalel is not a specific individual. He represents all of humanity. We are all made in God's image, endowed with *ru'akh Elohim*, the Divine spirit that enables us to envision and craft beauty, form and order out of the unformed stuff of creation.

That is, if we think of God as an infinitely creative artist—a force that shapes galaxies and worlds and molecules and atoms out of the building blocks of the universe—then we humans, created in the image of that master craftsman, are also endowed with these extraordinary abilities. To be made *b'tzelem Elohim* is to be able to shape the raw materials of our world into new forms. We create delicious meals, beautiful buildings, powerful technologies, breathtaking music and art. We also take the raw ingredients of relationships and can craft them either into vessels of love or cruelty. We create social orders that either support each person to realize their own Divine potential, or suppress and dehumanize them instead.

Betzalel's lineage tells us much more about how the Torah envisions a human being who consciously embraces his or her Divine nature:

בְּצַלְאֵל Betzalel: "In God's image"

בֶּן אוּרִי son of Uri: "My Light"

בֶּן־חוּר son of Hur: "Free" or "Noble"

לְמַטֵּה יְהוּדָה of the tribe of Yehuda: "I give thanks to God."

Betzalel's (or our) full, royal name is Made in God's Image, Child of My Light, Noble and Free, of the tribe of Gratitude.

As the book of Exodus comes to a close, we are reminded that we are endowed with *ru'akh Elohim*—a Divine spirit of wisdom, skill and knowledge in all manner of craft. We have been freed from bondage in order to realize our true, creative, noble and free nature. We have been freed from bondage in order to make our homes, our communities and our world into places alive with the hum of creative, not destructive, energy. Betzalel is each of us, every day, making a space in our hearts and in our homes where beauty, love and a sense of the infinite can dwell.

ויקרא
Leviticus

ואהבת לרעך כמוך אני יהוה
Love your neighbor as yourself: I am YHVH.
(Leviticus 19:18)

24 ——————————

Vayikra | ויקרא

Leviticus as Literature

וַיִּקְרָא אֶל־מֹשֶׁה וַיְדַבֵּר יְהוָה אֵלָיו מֵאֹהֶל מוֹעֵד

Va'yikra el Moshe va'yedabeir YHVH eilav mei'ohel mo'eid

YHVH called to Moses, and spoke to him from the Tent of
Meeting (Leviticus 1:1).

FOR THE MODERN READER, the book of Leviticus appears to be an odd
and even unwelcome intrusion into the grand saga of our ancestors. After
the satisfying conclusion of the book of Exodus, in which the Children of
Israel have reunited with their God, we are ready to hear about their further adventures on the way to the Promised Land. Instead, the action stops,
and we find ourselves wading through an entire book describing the arcane
practices and requirements of the *kohanim*, the priestly caste who maintain
the holy sanctuary that travels with the Children of Israel on their journeys.

But what if the Torah—the Five Books of Moses—is not organized
into the narrative shape to which we modern readers are accustomed?
This is the argument of the great anthropologist Mary Douglas (1921-
2007). Douglas may be best known for her work *Purity and Danger: An*

Analysis of Concepts of Pollution and Taboo (1966). In that groundbreaking work, Douglas included an examination of the concept of ritual purity in Leviticus. Douglas remained fascinated with Leviticus and in her retirement composed *Leviticus as Literature* (1999), a brilliant interweaving of anthropology and biblical criticism. Douglas argues that Leviticus, like many famous ancient texts, is misunderstood because the literary style in which it was written is unfamiliar today. She makes a compelling case that if we grasp the literary structure of Leviticus and the Torah as a whole, a complex, yet elegant and coherent, picture emerges into our view.

RING COMPOSITION

What if some forms of ancient literature are built on a structure that places their climax in the middle, rather than at the end of the book? Douglas calls this form "ring composition." She has us imagine a pediment—the triangular stone engraved with carvings that sits atop columns in classic Greek architecture. The carvings tell a story, with the climax at the apex of the triangle. The columns supporting either end of the pediment compare to the beginning and ending sections of the literary form. These pillars balance each other while supporting the centerpiece of the text. What if the Torah is structured in an analogous way, with the first two and final two books acting as columns upon which is perched Leviticus, the centerpiece of the Torah?

In this reading, we can understand the Torah as asking a central question throughout: How do we make a home for God in our midst? What does it mean to be a גּוֹי קָדוֹשׁ *goy kadosh*, a holy community? If the Torah is a ring composition, rather than strictly a linear narrative, then Leviticus as the central book of the five books of the Torah is not some detour from our story. Just as the *Mishkan* sits at the center of the Israelite camp and houses the Divine Presence, Leviticus sits at the center of our Torah and houses the teachings and instructions to maintain that *Mishkan*. The opening verse of Leviticus alerts us to our theme: "YHVH called to Moses, and spoke to him from the Tent of Meeting." The Children of Israel must maintain this Tent of Meeting so that God can dwell among them, and Leviticus will instruct them how.

ANALOGICAL THINKING

But this awareness does not make the ensuing instructions any less opaque to a modern reader. For what follows are chapters upon chapters of instructions regarding animal sacrifices and ritual purity that don't seem to follow a logical pattern. What kind of instruction manual is this? To the modern reader, the purpose of these practices—not to mention the specificity of detail with which they are described—is mystifying. Mary Douglas insists that our handicap is that we moderns are trained to think logically, but not analogically; linearly, rather than associatively. Modern thought is based on rational and logical reasoning. This emphasis has allowed us to realize mind-boggling technological advances in our era with no end in sight. We are accustomed to an instruction manual that will tell us how to assemble a piece of furniture or write code for a computer.

The problem is that Leviticus is an instruction manual for experiencing the presence of God in our midst, and that project will not yield to our logical inquiry alone. That project demands a different kind of thinking, one that perceives the connectivity and interrelation of everything. We might call this the poetic mind or perhaps the "right brain," or, as Douglas expresses it, analogical thinking. In such thinking, every aspect of reality can be seen as an analogy for every other aspect; the human body is a microcosm of human society, which is a microcosm of the natural world, which is a microcosm of the movement of the stars and planets, ad infinitum. In analogical thinking, God is not a separate, distant and distinct overlord of creation. Rather, God is present in every relationship within the creation—from the sub-atomic to the celestial, and every combination in between. To make a home for God in our midst, we must recognize that everything is connected.

Douglas argues that ancient Israelite society saw all of creation as a map of analogies. For example, the peak of Mount Sinai, representing the place where heaven and earth touch, is where God's presence descended and hovered, and the place from which God speaks. The Torah describes that the ordinary Israelites were not permitted to ascend any part of the mountain, so they gathered around its base. The elders were permitted to ascend partway and behold the Divine Presence from that height. Only Moses could ascend all the way to the summit, there to disappear into the dusky cloud that rested there, commune with God and receive the Torah. By analogy, the Israelite camp is carefully arranged with a similar hierarchy, recreating in human communal structure the topography of holiness found at Sinai: The tribes of Israel camp in a circle around the outside of the sacred enclosure that sits at the center of the camp; they are not permitted to enter it. The Levite tribe now become the institutionalized equivalent of the elders; they are permitted into the outer enclosure of the sacred precinct and tasked with its upkeep.

The inner sanctum, known as the Holy of Holies, represents the peak of the mountain. It is shrouded by the smoke of incense, just as the mountaintop was shrouded by the cloud of God's presence. Within the Holy of Holies, in a special ark, rest the engraved tablets of the Law that Moses brought down from the mountaintop. Aaron, the High Priest, now fulfills Moses's role, and is the only one permitted to enter the Holy of Holies. Aaron wears vestments that make him the symbolic representative of the entire people, carrying their names inscribed on his shoulders and over his heart, bringing the entire people near to God. As the peak of Mount Sinai was the place where heaven and earth could touch, so the Holy of Holies is now the earthly analogue of that sublime interface.

Another example: the Hebrew word for sacrifice is קָרְבָּן *korban,* meaning "drawing near." The purpose of the קָרְבָּנוֹת *korbanot,* the animal offerings, is to bring the person making the offering nearer to God—to restore connection to the Divine source. This was no mere barbecue. It was a symbolic offering up, a drawing near, of that person's best and purest self. Douglas ingeniously describes how even the most arcane details about which parts of the animal's innards are washed, put on the altar or saved for consumption can be read as yet another symbolic map of relationship between humans and the Divine.

Douglas includes not only the content of Leviticus in her map of analogies, but the literary structure of the book itself. Just as the Holy of Holies is at the very center of the Israelite camp, just as the pinnacle of the Holy Mountain is covered with the Cloud of Glory, just as the innermost parts of the animal are offered up on the altar, so the center of Leviticus represents the Holy of Holies of the Torah text. The center of Leviticus—the book that is the center of the Five Books of Moses—would figuratively be the apex of the pediment, the climax of the story, the place closest to God. And the center of Leviticus is the portion known as *Kedoshim*: The Holiness Laws. Here, the text turns from ritual instruction to moral code. If the Children of Israel are going to create a society in which God's presence can dwell, then they must recognize that every human is a microcosm of the Divine and treat humans with the reverence that is their innate due. If we cannot create a moral society, then we will never create a dwelling place for God in our midst.

So, at the very peak, or, shall we say, the very heart of the Torah comes this instruction:

> וְאָהַבְתָּ לְרֵעֲךָ כָּמוֹךָ *V'ahavta l'rei'ekha kamokha*—Love your neighbor as yourself (Leviticus 19:18).

As Rabbi Akiva taught, this is the כְּלָל גָּדוֹל בַּתּוֹרָה *k'lal gadol baTorah*—the central principle of the Torah, its Holy of Holies. The entire edifice of Torah builds up to, and is built around, this verse.

Mary Douglas has persuaded me that the Torah is truly an ancient literary masterpiece, form and function aligned, teaching us how to build our lives into a home for godliness.

25 ————————————

Tzav | צו

The Haftarah as Commentary and Critique

וַיְדַבֵּר יְהוָה אֶל־מֹשֶׁה לֵּאמֹר: צַו אֶת־אַהֲרֹן וְאֶת־בָּנָיו לֵאמֹר
זֹאת תּוֹרַת הָעֹלָה . . .

*Va'yedabeir YHVH el Moshe lei'mor: Tzav et Aharon
v'et banav lei'mor: Zot torat ha'olah . . .*

And YHVH spoke to Moses, saying: Command Aaron and his
sons thus: These are the instructions for the burnt offering . . .
(Leviticus 6:1–2).

This is what YHVH Almighty, the God of Israel, says: Go ahead,
add your burnt offerings to your other sacrifices and eat the
meat yourselves! For when I brought your ancestors out of
Egypt and spoke to them, I did not that day give them commands about burnt offerings and sacrifices, but I gave them this
command: Obey me, and I will be your God and you will be my
people. Walk in the way that I enjoin upon you, that it may go
well with you (Haftarah of Tzav, Jeremiah 7: 21–23).

FOR AT LEAST 2,000 years, the weekly Torah reading has been accompanied by an excerpt from the section of the Hebrew Bible known as the prophets. This reading is called the הַפְטָרָה Haftarah (or הַפְטוֹרָה *Haftorah*, with the Yiddish inflection). Haftarah means "conclusion" or "completion." It concludes or completes the Torah reading.

The origin of this practice is unknown, although theories abound. What we do know is that these Prophetic passages were chosen deliberately as commentary on the given Torah portion. Sometimes, the Haftarah amplifies the message of the Torah portion; sometimes, it critiques that message. This is a classic method of rabbinic Torah commentary; when the rabbis took issue with some aspect of Torah they found problematic, they would find passages from elsewhere in the Bible to make their point. In this way, they would not be seen as actively disagreeing with the sacred text, but could still express their view by letting the Bible critique itself. The rabbis were in good company, for the prophets in their own era (10th- to fourth-centuries BCE) established the Jewish norm that self-critique was a necessary component of sacred discourse.

I have found, therefore, that reading the Haftarah portion as a form of rabbinic commentary on its accompanying Torah portion is a very fruitful approach. The Haftarah of *Tzav* is an excellent example.

The entire portion of *Tzav* is a detailed description about the proper way in which to offer sacrifices to God: the different kinds of offerings, the way to prepare them, which parts may be eaten and by whom. As alien as these rituals appear to us today, it is not difficult to imagine the power they held for our ancestors. Rituals can focus our attention and can be filled with meaning—think of the power of a beautiful wedding ceremony and the importance that we invest in it. But rituals can also devolve into rote performance, and the meaning and inspiration that they are meant to evoke can easily be lost.

This was as true in ancient times as it is today. The sacrifices of our Torah portion were meant to symbolize a person's inner transformation. A sin offering was meant to be accompanied by, and to reinforce, a feeling of repentance. A burnt offering might evoke awe and closeness to God. A thanksgiving offering was to awaken gratitude.

But the prophets repeatedly castigated the Israelites for thinking that the sacrifices were an end in themselves, and that God was content with food offerings on the altar. This was not the message of the God who spoke at Mount Sinai, who commanded us to love justice and mercy, and to care for the weak! The rabbis had little difficulty finding prophetic passages that speak to the Jewish imperative to elevate moral behavior over ritual performance.

Here is a classic example from the Prophet Micah 6:6–8:

> With what shall I come before YHVH and bow down before the exalted God? Shall I come before YHVH with burnt offerings, with calves a year old? Will YHVH be pleased with thousands of rams, with ten thousand rivers of olive oil? Shall I offer my first-born for my transgression, the fruit of my body for the sin of my soul? No, YHVH has shown you, O mortal, what is good and what YHVH requires of you: To act justly and to love mercy and to walk humbly with your God.

The rabbis inherited this tradition from the prophets, and they codified it into Jewish law: sacrifice, prayer and all forms of worship have no value unless the heart is directed towards heaven. The outer performance of rituals must be approached as actions that awaken the inner self.

Addressing this week's Torah portion, the rabbis express this imperative by choosing the words of Jeremiah (cited at the top of this essay) as the Haftarah. They even have the audacity to patch together two separate passages from Jeremiah: 7:21–8:3 and 9:22–23. They were clearly willing to reshuffle passages from the Bible in order to strengthen their own interpretation. Speaking in the sixth century BCE, Jeremiah makes the rhetorical point that when the Children of Israel first heard God speak at Mount Sinai, there was no mention of sacrifices. The first words they heard at the holy mountain were to obey YHVH, to honor Shabbat, to not steal or murder or lie or covet. Only later do they receive the instructions regarding sacrifices, thus indicating their lesser importance in the hierarchy of God's desires for us.

The rabbis are determined to remind us that as we immerse ourselves in Leviticus—the book of the Torah that is preoccupied with the details of ritual performance—we not forget the true purpose of these rituals. God wants something much more difficult and much more exalting from us: to ignite, to tend and to offer to the world our inner fire of righteousness, kindness and awe. And so, they conclude the Haftarah with these inspiring words from Jeremiah 9:22–23:

> Thus says YHVH, Life Unfolding: Let not the wise glory in their wisdom, let not the mighty glory in their might, let not the rich glory in their riches; Rather let them who glory, glory in this; that

they understand and know Me, that I, YHVH, practice kindness, justice, and righteousness on the earth; it is in these things that I delight, says YHVH.

26 ————————————

Shemini | שמיני

What Happened to Nadav and Avihu?

וַיִּקְחוּ בְנֵי־אַהֲרֹן נָדָב וַאֲבִיהוּא אִישׁ מַחְתָּתוֹ וַיִּתְּנוּ בָהֵן אֵשׁ
וַיָּשִׂימוּ עָלֶיהָ קְטֹרֶת וַיַּקְרִיבוּ לִפְנֵי יְהֹוָה אֵשׁ זָרָה אֲשֶׁר לֹא
צִוָּה אֹתָם: וַתֵּצֵא אֵשׁ מִלִּפְנֵי יְהֹוָה וַתֹּאכַל אוֹתָם וַיָּמֻתוּ לִפְנֵי
יְהֹוָה:

*Va'yik'khu v'nei Aharon, Nadav v'Avihu, ish
makhtato va'yitnu va'hein eish va'yasimu aleha ketoret
va'yakrivu lifnei YHVH eish zarah asher lo tzivah
otam. Va'teitzei eish milifnei YHVH va'tokhal otam
va'yamutu lifnei YHVH.*

Now Aaron's sons, Nadav and Avihu, each took his incense
pan, put fire and incense in them, and brought near to the
presence of YHVH unauthorized fire, that had not been
prescribed. And fire came forth from the presence of YHVH
and consumed them, and they died in the presence of YHVH
(Leviticus 10:1–2).

THIS IS ONE OF the most mystifying passages in the Torah. Why are Nadav and Avihu consumed by YHVH's fire? Moses and Aaron's response only adds to the mystery:

> Then Moses said to Aaron, "This is what YHVH spoke of, saying: 'Through those who draw near to Me, I will be made holy, In the presence of the entire people, I will be glorified.'" And Aaron was silent (Leviticus 10:3).

Why does Moses express no sympathy or grief? Why is Aaron silent? What is their understanding of the import of these deaths?

Moses instructs Aaron's two remaining sons to carry the bodies of their brothers outside of the camp. YHVH then addresses Aaron directly and instructs him that he and his sons should never be intoxicated when entering the Tent of Meeting.

We should also note that immediately prior to Nadav and Avihu's fatal trespass, the entire people had witnessed the Glory of YHVH, from which a fire descended onto the altar, and consumed the offering that Aaron and Moses had elaborately and precisely prepared. The Torah tells us, "the entire people saw, and shouted aloud, and flung themselves on their faces!" (Leviticus 9:24).

We are perhaps given clues as to why Nadav and Avihu were consumed by the holy fire, but no direct explanation. Were they intoxicated? Were they insufficiently respectful of the power of the Divine Presence? The simplest reading of the passage seems to indicate that Nadav and Avihu's death was a punishment for their transgression, and an object lesson in the ways to properly worship God. This is certainly how many Torah commentators read this story: Beware, this is what happens if you don't follow the rules! Don't play with fire!

There is obvious value in that lesson, but if we end our inquiry there, we once again underestimate the Torah. The Torah is always teaching us about our spiritual quest, as well as our social and moral development. Stories about our interactions with YHVH are meant to be understood metaphorically; they point to a spiritual reality that can only be hinted at in concrete descriptions. Elsewhere in Torah are clues that give us a deeper understanding of Nadav and Avihu's fate.

We find Nadav and Avihu singled out in an earlier passage in Exodus:

> Then Moses and Aaron, Nadav and Avihu, and seventy elders of Israel ascended [Mount Sinai], and they beheld the God of Israel,

under whose feet was the likeness of a pavement of sapphire, like the very sky in its purity. Yet God did not raise a hand against these leaders of Israel; rather, they beheld God, and they ate and drank (Exodus 24:9–11).

In this remarkable passage, Nadav and Avihu are privileged to join in the most sublime mystical experience: to behold God. This was no ordinary picnic! Rather, some commentators suggest, the leaders of Israel were imbibing God's Presence, sating their spiritual rather than their physical hunger. And what a vision it is—sapphire and sky blue, clarity and pure bliss! As the psalmist says, "One thing I ask of YHVH, only one thing do I seek: that I might dwell in YHVH's house and behold with delight the Divine Presence" (Psalm 27:4).

As a mystical and visionary text, the Torah speaks to that desire to directly experience the unfiltered glory of the universe. Mystics from varied cultures and epochs describe this as an experience of oneness, during which one's individual identity becomes insignificant and even disappears, accompanied by a longing to dissolve separateness entirely and merge forever with this sublime mystery. How does one return to ordinary consciousness after experiencing this transcendence? How does one reconcile the coarseness and suffering of everyday life with Divine bliss?

Moses and Aaron are able to live with this dissonance, or paradox, of awareness. This is what makes them great spiritual leaders and teachers. Moses can come back down from the mountaintop and bring that illuminating wisdom to the world. Aaron can enter the Holy of Holies, and yet emerge whole to minister to and to bless the people. As adepts, they understand that during our discrete lifetimes on earth, we somehow must simultaneously live in two realms: the realm of sublime oneness, of holy fire that illuminates all of creation; and the realm of twoness, self *and* other, light *and* dark, good *and* evil, life *and* death. As adepts, Moses and Aaron understand that their task while in the land of the living is to resist the temptation to merge with the light, and instead to translate all the light and power and glory of that level of perception into loving and righteous acts in our broken, needy and confounding world. This is one way of describing what Jewish tradition means when it asks us to be "partners with God."

Nadav and Avihu appear to be of a different ilk. Perhaps after their experience with their father and uncle and the elders on Mount Sinai, their longing to return to that bliss never left them. Now, in this week's Torah portion, the Tent of Meeting has finally been completed. God's glorious

Presence, beheld last at Mount Sinai, has once again been invoked, and the people react with awe and trembling and exultation. Perhaps Nadav and Avihu cannot restrain their enthusiasm. (In fact, enthusiasm literally means "filled with God"—all that Nadav and Avihu want is to be filled with God.) They enter the Holy of Holies uninvited and unprepared, and offer themselves to the Oneness of mystical union. And they do not return. Perhaps their death is not a punishment, but simply a consequence of their overwhelming desire to be with the light, to the exclusion of their attachments to this world of broken vessels. Perhaps, from their perspective, their death is not even a death, but a blissful return. Perhaps we will all reach this destination one day and finally understand that our fears of death were unfounded.

But in the meantime, the Torah instructs Aaron that henceforth, no one should enter the Tent of Meeting in an intoxicated state. Again, I think this is a metaphor for spiritual rather than physical intoxication. One can be so "God-intoxicated" that when entering the rarified realm of the Tent of Meeting, one could lose one's bearings, drunk with Divine love. One could become confused and think that our purpose and goal is to remain in this dissociated state, rather than to remember and understand that the purpose of this bliss is not for self-satiation, but to become a channel of blessing so that one can be a source of satiation to others. To be a source of blessing to the world, one must learn to remain simultaneously grounded and elevated, bridging both realms. Nadav and Avihu never learned how to keep their feet on the ground. As a result, they were "blown away" by the holy fire. It was not their bodies that were consumed by that metaphorical flame, but their souls.

The tale of Nadav and Avihu is indeed a cautionary one, but I think it is especially directed to spiritual seekers. Judaism does not privilege the spiritual realm over the physical realm. Or, as one might say in more traditional God-language: God didn't create the world in order for us to transcend it, but that we might bring godliness into it. As Rabbi Larry Kushner expresses it in one of my favorite passages from his classic book on Jewish spirituality, *Honey From the Rock* (p. 134):

> And such indeed is the mark of any would-be Jewish spirituality:
> that the way to God only comes through religious doing. And that
> religious doing can only occur in this world. And for this reason,
> this world is holy, too. For some searchers it is a necessary evil,
> something to cast off. For us it is the only way of ascending to

other worlds. It is not a stumbling block or obstacle that must be avoided. It is the very way itself. It is not our way, our goal as the children of Jacob, to leave this world of broken vessels and misplaced love. But rather to go out to it.

27 —————————————————————————

Tazri'a | תזריע

The Meaning of Forty

אִשָּׁה כִּי תַזְרִיעַ וְיָלְדָה . . .

Isha ki tazri'a v'yaldah . . .

When a woman conceives and give birth . . . (Leviticus 12:2).

OUR PORTION BEGINS WITH a chapter that, at eight verses, happens to be the shortest chapter in the Torah. Chapter 12 describes the extended period after childbirth, during which a woman is considered ritually impure.

I know that many of us have an immediate and negative reaction to this instruction: Sexist! How could childbirth make a woman impure? And furthermore, the Torah tells us that while a woman must remain in this condition of impurity for 40 days for a male child, if she bears a daughter, she must endure 80 days. Is she being punished for bearing a female child? While our contemporary understanding of the workings of sexism in human culture is revolutionary and transformative, our assumptions can also cloud our analysis. The culture of ancient Israel was radically different from our own, and it behooves us to seek to understand that culture on its own terms.

In the Torah, it is not gender that makes one ritually impure; it is the presence of blood. Blood is the life force made visible. Blood is powerful and dangerous. Blood, as the life force, comes from God and therefore is holy and belongs to God.

When an animal is slaughtered, whether for ritual sacrifice or for ordinary consumption, the Torah is unequivocal in its demand that the blood belongs to God and cannot be consumed: כִּי הַדָּם הוּא הַנֶּפֶשׁ וְלֹא־תֹאכַל הַנֶּפֶשׁ עִם־הַבָּשָׂר *Ki ha'dam hu ha'nefesh, v'lo tokhal ha'nefesh im ha'basar*—"For the blood is the soul, the life force; you are forbidden from eating the soul with the flesh." (Deuteronomy 12:23, one of many such instructions in the Torah. This is why to this day kosher meat must have the blood drained from the flesh.) When an animal is slaughtered, the Torah instructs that the blood (דָּם *dam*) must be poured backed into the earth (אֲדָמָה *adamah*). The connected sound of these two Hebrew words, *dam* and *adamah,* is not accidental. After Cain slays his brother, Abel, God adjures Cain: קוֹל דְּמֵי אָחִיךָ צֹעֲקִים אֵלַי מִן־הָאֲדָמָה *Kol d'mei akhikha tzo'akim eilai min ha'adamah*—"Your brother's blood cries out to me from the earth" (Genesis 4:10). I should also note that the Hebrew word for "human being" is אָדָם *adam*; when God creates Adam, the Torah tells us, "and God took earth—*adamah*—and made the *adam.* In God's likeness and image was the *adam* created." Thus, we see the linguistic connection that makes the earth, human beings and blood all sacred to the Creator: *dam, adam* and *adamah.*

When blood pours out of the body, therefore, one enters a liminal, dangerous zone; the sacred life force is exposed and must be treated with the greatest deference and care. Childbirth and women's menstrual cycles are included in this category. The menstrual cycle is especially awesome and mysterious—linked to the moon, which itself cycles between appearance and disappearance; blood flowing, and yet a sign of life and not death; and the cycle ceasing during gestation as life grows within. It is self-evident that women have a unique connection to the Source of Life.

The Torah's term for the category I translated above as "ritually impure" is טָמֵא *tamei,* and this is how *tamei* is usually rendered. *Tamei* is also often translated as "defiled." The problem with these translations is that, for contemporary readers, they evoke moral categories. "Impure" and "defiled" bring up images of moral failings and harsh judgments. That is not the intention of the biblical Hebrew. Therefore, Baruch Levine, in his commentary on Leviticus, suggests that we translate *tamei* as "susceptible."

The mother and her newborn are susceptible, in a danger zone, and need time to recuperate—not just physically, but spiritually—before being reintegrated into the community, before being able to re-enter the holy precinct of the Sanctuary.

Rather than a punishment for being female, what if in the mindset of ancient Israel, this time of "susceptibility" was a protection for being female, for being the gender that opens its body and brings forth new life, an ability that in the ancient world was not only awe-inspiring and miraculous, but also often fatal. Without mothers, the community would obviously not survive; still, pregnancy and childbirth were like walking a tightrope with no net—the odds of disaster were terribly high. Every birth was also a brush with death.

So the Torah set a lengthy period of time during which the new mother was considered to be in a state of טֻמְאָה *tum'ah*, "susceptibility." For a male child, the period was 40 days, and for a female child, 80 days. At the end of that period, the mother would bring an offering to the Tent of Meeting, and the priest would declare her once again to be in a state of טָהֳרָה *Tohorah*, ritual purity. The woman—with a healthy, growing baby in her arms—would now fully re-enter the life of the community.

But I have always wondered, why the number "40"? We know it well: the rains of Noah's flood fall 40 days and 40 nights; Moses stays on Mount Sinai 40 days and 40 nights; and most famously, the Children of Israel are made to wander 40 years in the Wilderness before they can enter the Promised Land. There are many other examples in the Torah. Given the primarily symbolic use of numbers throughout the Hebrew Bible, 40 is meant to represent something. But what?

A pregnancy. A due date was and still is calculated as 40 weeks from the first day of a woman's last menstrual period. Even though we now know that conception takes place about two weeks after the onset of the last period, the observable start date is that last period itself. And from that day, the average duration until the child is born is 40 weeks.

So, 40 represents a time of conception, gestation and maturation until a new being is ready to be born. It is a time of metamorphosis. It is a hidden miracle unfolding. As the due date approaches, it's also a time of constriction, struggle and convulsive pain, followed by liberation. No wonder the Children of Israel must wander for 40 years before they can pass through the Jordan River (birth canal?) into the Promised Land. They must shed their identity as Pharaoh's slaves and instead be reconceived, gestate and grow over a full term before they can be born anew as a free people in their own land. And the labor pains are tremendous—just read the travails in the book of Numbers!

This would explain why a new mother is restricted (or perhaps protected) for 40 days after the birth of a son: one day for each week of pregnancy, a symbolic correlation during which she becomes reintegrated into the life of the community. The question remains, however, why the period is doubled to 80 days when the baby is a girl? Although we might initially think that this is a punitive measure, what if instead it is an acknowledgment of the life-giving power of women? In this case, a birth-giver has given birth to a future birth-giver. The new baby girl will mature and one day enter that same intimate relationship with blood, the essence of life, and she will gain the ability to be a life-giver herself. And today, we know that baby girls are born with all of their future eggs already nestled in their ovaries. Future life is already contained in the newborn girl.

Perhaps, then, the double period of 80 days mandated after the birth of a girl-child is not punitive, but rather an acknowledgement that a new life-giver has been born, and 40 additional days of waiting might help to "inoculate" this baby against the dangers she will one day navigate as she brings the next generation into the world. For women are indeed God-like in their ability to bring forth new life. They bear a mysterious, awesome and dangerous power. Men and women both are intimate with the life-sapping potential of blood flowing from our bodies, and the Torah requires both men and women to go through a period of susceptibility, and then reintegration when they contact the realm that might lead to death. But only women become intimate with the life-giving potential of the blood that flows from their bodies. When that flow temporarily ceases for 40 weeks, the miracle of a new soul grows in their womb. Women have the capacity to be intimate with YHVH, Life Unfolding, in a way that men will never experience or understand.

28 ——————————————————

Metzora | מצרע
Body as Temple

וַיְדַבֵּר יְהֹוָה אֶל־מֹשֶׁה לֵּאמֹר: זֹאת תִּהְיֶה תּוֹרַת הַמְּצֹרָע בְּיוֹם
טָהֳרָתוֹ

*Va'yedabeir YHVH el Moshe lei'mor: zot tih'yeh torat
ha'metzora b'yom tohorato*

YHVH said to Moses: "This is the Torah (instruction) for the
person with the skin affliction so that they may be restored to
wholeness" (Leviticus 14:1).

METZORA IS AMONG THE most obscure sections of the Torah. *Metzora*,
along with the latter chapters of the preceding portion *Tazri'a*, describes
a variety of physical symptoms that make a person temporarily unfit to
be close to God, and the rituals required in order to restore that person
to fitness. From our modern rational perspective, these chapters appear to
be some strange and primitive medical manual. But as I have previously
explained, to understand Leviticus we must apply metaphor and analogy
more than logic.

The world, the human community and the human body can all be
dwelling places for the Divine glory. The difference between these realms

111

is that while it is a relatively simple matter to perceive the Divine glory in the natural world, continual effort is required to maintain human society in a manner that allows us to sense that glory and presence in our midst. Human society can easily become debased, a place of darkness and evil. God's presence in our midst is not a given. The task of the Children of Israel is to maintain a society in which that Divine glory can be felt and perceived: "You shall be holy, for I, YHVH, am holy" (Leviticus 19:2). "Build me a holy dwelling, that I might dwell in your midst" (Exodus 25:8). "You shall be a nation of priests, a holy people" (Exodus 19:6). If the Children of Israel, individually and collectively, can make their humanly wrought society a fitting dwelling place for the Divine presence, they will then align themselves with God's creation, in which the Divine presence already overflows. As above, so below: We will be manifesting our true potential as beings made in the image of God.

What does "holy" mean? In English, holy derives from the Old English word that also gives us "whole" and "heal." Holiness is wholeness. In order to be a dwelling place for God, we must be whole. We must have integrity. The Hebrew term for "holy" is קָדוֹשׁ *kadosh* and has similar associations. That which is *kadosh* is able to house the Divine presence. The opposite of *kadosh* is חָלָל *halal*, the root of which means "desecrate," but literally refers to openings or punctures. Thus, both the Hebrew and English root words tell us that if one's moral integrity is compromised (if one's container is leaky, as it were), one is unable to house the Divine presence.

Tazri'a and *Metzora* describe conditions in which integrity is damaged, and manifests as a physical set of symptoms. The Torah calls this condition *tzara'at*. *Tzara'at*, which has been incorrectly rendered into English as "leprosy," derives from the same root as *metzora*; the מְצֹרָע *metzora* is the person who suffers from צָרַעַת *tzara'at*. *Tzara'at* can afflict a person, a garment or even a house. It breaks up the integrity of the skin of the body, or the cloth of a garment, or the walls of a house with discoloration. Metaphorically *tzara'at* appears to be an outer manifestation of inner loss of integrity. The body, the home or the community, rather than maintaining a secure dwelling place for Divine energy, has become leaky and drafty, unable to host the Divine Presence. There must be a way to heal and to recover from this spiritual ailment so that a person may rejoin the holy community.

It is interesting to note that ancient rabbinic commentators also assign a metaphoric meaning to this affliction. Using wordplay, the rabbis rework מְצֹרָע *metzora*—the person afflicted with this spiritual disorder—into

מוֹצִיא רָע *motzi rah*, which means one who draws out the bad. In the rabbinic telling, a person who is a *metzora* has habitually spoken in hurtful ways: slander, tale-bearing, rumor-mongering—that is, any use of language that can damage or destroy another's reputation. For the rabbis, *tzara'at* is the physical symptom of a spiritual disease. The *metzora* draws out the bad rather than the good, using language to break down rather than build up. We could say that this person has "loose lips" and cannot contain himself adequately. But "I couldn't contain myself" is never an adequate excuse. Conscience, empathy and thinking before one speaks are all necessary preconditions for the experience of holiness. Those who "leak" harmful words have lost their integrity. Holiness and wholeness have been lost, and the Divine presence cannot manifest there.

According to Leviticus, the *metzora*, the one afflicted with *tzara'at*, must leave the camp and wait seven days. This does not appear to be a punishment, but rather, a treatment. We might even speculate that this period outside the camp is an opportunity for reflection, a retreat of sorts. The כֹּהֵן *kohein* (which means "priest"), whose role is to maintain the dwelling place for God in the Israelite camp, carefully inspects the *metzora* to see if they have healed. If their skin is uniform once again, the *kohein* leads them through an elaborate ritual of reintegration into the community. The ritual includes an offering to God. The Hebrew term for offering is קָרְבָּן *korban*, which means "drawing near." Healed and whole, the individual is now able to be intimate with God once more.

Again, metaphorically, we might say that an inner state of disconnection or fragmentation has been resolved, and focus and energy have been restored. If our energy and attention are distracted, leaking, dissipated, we cannot remain aware of or address the great majesty and mystery in which we dwell and which dwells within each of us. The *kohein* might be thought of as the spiritual healer who examines us carefully and guides us back into connection with the Divine.

I invite you to think about the ways you restore a sense of wholeness to yourself when you feel fragmented or feel that you have damaged your integrity. As you restore your inner focus—and as you take any external actions you determine necessary to make amends and restore wholeness to yourself and to your relationships—may you experience the grace, the goodness and the speechless awe that comes with the awareness of being filled with Life Unfolding.

29 ─────────────────────────────

Akharei Mot | אחרי מות

The First Yom Kippur

וְהָיְתָה לָכֶם לְחֻקַּת עוֹלָם בַּחֹדֶשׁ הַשְּׁבִיעִי בֶּעָשׂוֹר לַחֹדֶשׁ
תְּעַנּוּ אֶת־נַפְשֹׁתֵיכֶם וְכָל־מְלָאכָה לֹא תַעֲשׂוּ הָאֶזְרָח וְהַגֵּר
הַגָּר בְּתוֹכְכֶם: כִּי־בַיּוֹם הַזֶּה יְכַפֵּר עֲלֵיכֶם לְטַהֵר אֶתְכֶם מִכֹּל
חַטֹּאתֵיכֶם

*V'ha'ytah la'khem l'khukat olam: ba'khodesh
ha'shvi'i be'asor lakhodesh t'anu et nafshoteikhem,
v'khol melakhah lo ta'asu, ha'ezrakh v'hageir hagar
b'tokhakhem. Ki va'yom ha'zeh y'khapeir aleikhem
l'taheir etkhem mikol hatoteikhem*

And this shall be for you a law for all time: In the seventh
month, on the tenth day of the month, you shall practice
self-denial, and you shall do no manner of work, neither the
citizen nor the stranger who dwells among you. For on this
day atonement shall be made for you, to cleanse you of all
your sins (Leviticus 16:29–30).

CHAPTER 16 OF THIS week's portion describes in detail how to enact Yom Kippur: dressed in plain white linen (as opposed to his regular very elaborate vestments), Aaron, הַכֹּהֵן הַגָּדוֹל *ha'Kohein ha'Gadol*, the High Priest, enters the sanctuary alone and sacrifices a bull and a ram. Then he takes two goats and casts lots upon them. One goat is slaughtered and offered to God on behalf of the people's sins. The other goat is chosen as the scapegoat. (This biblical goat is, in fact, the origin of the English term "scapegoat." In Hebrew, the term is שְׂעִיר לַעֲזָאזֵל *s'ir l'azazeil*, a whole other fascinating story, for another time.) Aaron lays his hands on the scapegoat, confessing all the sins of the people and transferring them onto the goat. The goat is then sent away into the wilderness, carrying the people's sins away with it. The people are now purified of their transgressions so that God can continue to dwell in their midst. At the end of the description, the Torah announces, "And this shall be for you a law for all time."

What's wrong with this picture?

Well, thousands of years later, we are still marking the tenth day of the seventh month, Yom Kippur, as a day when we practice self-denial and seek atonement for our sins. That much is consistent—miraculously so. But we practice none of the ritual described in the Torah: no High Priest, no animal sacrifice, no Holy of Holies, no scapegoat. All of these practices ceased after the Second Temple was destroyed in 70 C.E. Yom Kippur today resembles the Yom Kippur of the Torah in no way at all.

This makes Yom Kippur a signal example of Rabbi Mordecai Kaplan's description of Judaism as the evolving religious civilization of the Jewish People. Through numerous disruptive historical, geographical and cultural upheavals and transformations, we Jews have succeeded in retaining the inner meaning and purpose of the Day of Atonement. The outer form has evolved so dramatically that a contemporary Yom Kippur would be unrecognizable to our biblical forebears. Over time, prayers replaced animal sacrifices; communal confession replaced the work of the High Priest; fasting, which is not explicitly prescribed in the Torah, became the central accepted form of "self-denial"; synagogues replaced the *mishkan* and its Holy of Holies; the compelling ritual of the scapegoat has long since disappeared (we still read about it on Yom Kippur, but no longer enact it) and has been superseded by the rabbinic commandment that the ritual of Yom Kippur does not atone for wrongdoing unless one has already attempted to reconcile with the people one has wronged. And you might notice that rabbis weren't even invented back then!

Our longevity as a people is not a result of our unwillingness to change. On the contrary, we are still here precisely because of our ability to evolve and adapt to changing circumstances, while still retaining the life-sustaining teachings of our ancient roots.

We draw this same lesson when we compare the Festival of Passover as it is described in Torah to Passover celebrations today. Readers of the Torah are always surprised to discover that there is no mention of a Passover Seder in the Torah, yet the Seder is the central feature of the Passover observances that we know. The external form continues to evolve so that it can carry the timeless truth ever forward—that oppression and subjugation must give way to freedom.

The central message of Yom Kippur also has not wavered, despite (or perhaps as a result of) the evolving outer form of the Holy Day: We must be accountable for our actions; we must make amends for our misdeeds; when we feel separated from God and from one another, forgiveness and reconciliation are always possible. I picture our ancestors following that scapegoat with their eyes as it wandered out of sight into the wilderness. I imagine the relief and release they felt as they knew they had been offered a chance to begin again. I think of the way my entire congregation chants the confession of sins, and then we pour out our hearts singing and praying *Avinu Malkeinu* together, swaying as one, our hearts all aiming at that distant horizon, and I feel that same relief and release: We, too, can begin again.

What a marvelous paradox! The form must evolve so that Judaism can continue to reveal its timeless teachings to a changing world. Only in this way can the link to our Torah remain intact.

30

Kedoshim | קדשים

The Mitzvah of Tokhekha: *Tough Love*

לֹא־תִשְׂנָא אֶת־אָחִיךָ בִּלְבָבֶךָ הוֹכֵחַ תּוֹכִיחַ אֶת־עֲמִיתֶךָ
וְלֹא־תִשָּׂא עָלָיו חֵטְא:

*Lo tisna et akhikha bilvavekha; hokhei'akh tokhi'akh et
amitekha v'lo tisa alav heit.*

Do not hate your brother or sister in your heart; you must
admonish, yes, admonish them or you will bear some of their
sin (Leviticus 19:17).

THIS WEEK'S TORAH PORTION is named *Kedoshim*, derived from the
opening instruction of the parashah קְדשִׁים תִּהְיוּ *kedoshim tih'yu*—"You
shall be holy" (Leviticus 19:2). The verses that follow describe the ethical
and interpersonal behavior necessary to achieve this quality of holiness.
The instructions culminate in verse 18: וְאָהַבְתָּ לְרֵעֲךָ כָּמוֹךָ *V'ahavta l'rei'akha
kamokha*—"You shall love your neighbor as yourself."

Here is our Golden Rule. Yet how do we enact it? What actions and
attitudes must we practice to align ourselves with this ideal?

The answers lie precisely in the verses leading up to this declaration.
These instructions make clear that the love we are to show our neighbor is

117

not merely some generalized good will, but an active engagement in their well-being. The verse cited above, "Do not hate your brother or sister in your heart; you must admonish, yes, admonish them or you will bear some of their sin" immediately precedes the Golden Rule.

To love one's neighbor as oneself, one must be willing to admonish them when you see them missing the mark with their behavior. If you do not attempt to intervene, the Torah insists that you bear some measure of responsibility for their failures.

Now, of course, we are each ultimately responsible for our own behavior. But the Torah is clear that our task is to become a holy community, concerned with each other's welfare. We are our brother's keeper. How do we intervene when we see our brother or sister doing something that we know is wrong?

This is a challenge with no easy answer, a veritable minefield of wrong moves, as any of us who have tried to lovingly and thoughtfully intervene with a loved one knows all too well. But the Torah insists that it is our responsibility to try. Fortunately, centuries of wise Jewish commentators give us guidance on how to proceed:

Rabbi Yehudah Aryeh Leib, an early disciple of the Baal Shem Tov (c. 1760), was known as the "The Mokhiakh of Polonnoye." A מוֹכִיחַ *mokhiakh* is "one who rebukes." That is, R. Yehudah Aryeh Leib specialized in the art of rebuke. He notes that we must pay attention to the entire verse because the first half of the verse establishes the conditions necessary for the second half:

> The one who rebukes needs first of all to check himself, to see if there is any grudge or resentment in his heart, any negative or constricted feeling, regarding the person that he is about to rebuke. Only if it is clear to you that you "do not hate your brother in your heart" are you permitted to rebuke him.

Rabbi Alexander Zusia Friedman (Poland, 1899–1943) was murdered by the Nazis after the liquidation of the Warsaw Ghetto. Rabbi Friedman teaches on the same verse:

> What is the connection between the two parts of this verse, "do not hate" and "rebuke, yes, rebuke"? The explanation is that true rebuke is possible only with one whom we love, whose behavior touches our heart and whose path we desire to make better, like a parent who rebukes her own child. To the extent that a person is close to someone, the love is greater and the rebuke is more

serious. And rebuke that comes from love has greater influence. You cannot rebuke one whom you hate, and in any case the rebuke would have no effect. Only by means of "do not hate" is it possible to carry out "rebuke, yes rebuke."

Based on my study and reflection on Judaism's teachings about this difficult *mitzvah,* I have come up with some basic rules for practicing תּוֹכֵחָה *tokheikha,* or the art of gentle rebuke. Reflecting on "The Mokhiakh of Polonnoye" and Rabbi Friedman's teachings, we can articulate the first rule:

Rule No. 1: Be clear about your loving intentions. Only then may you proceed.

It was taught in the Baal Shem Tov's name that one must first give rebuke to oneself and only then to one's fellow—and then it will become clear that there is within oneself a bit of the other's wrongdoing. Read the end of verse 17, וְלֹא־תִשָּׂא עָלָיו חֵטְא *v'lo tisa alav heit,* not as "or you will bear some of their sin," but rather as "and don't put all the sin on them!"

Rule No. 2: Examine yourself for the same negative qualities or actions that you find yourself wishing to rebuke in others. Be humble in your efforts, not self-righteous.

The Rambam (Rabbi Moshe ben Maimon, also known as Maimonides, Egypt, 1135–1204) teaches that one is forbidden to embarrass or shame the sinner when you rebuke them for it is also a sin to shame someone, especially in public. The Rambam derives this rule from yet another reading of *v'lo tisa alav heit:* You will bring sin upon yourself if you rebuke your neighbor in a manner that shames or humiliates them.

Rule No. 3: Choose your words, your tone and the timing of your delivery so as to avoid shaming or humiliating the person you are trying to assist with your intervention. Consider speaking with them in private.

A problem: All of these righteous and well-intentioned cautions might cause us to never say anything, lest our motivations or execution be impure! Rabbi Akiva (Israel, second century) is quoted as saying, "In this generation, there is no one who knows how a rebuke ought to be worded."

Yet the Torah is emphatic as it repeats the command הוֹכֵחַ תּוֹכִיחַ *hokhei'akh tokhi'akh*—"rebuke, yes, rebuke." This is important. Love without honesty is anemic, even false. True friendship demands that we hold one another up to a high standard. Sometimes, you just have to get in your friend's face for their own good—and damn the consequences.

Our tradition looks to Abraham as our model. In Genesis, God is considering whether to destroy Sodom and Gomorrah for their sinfulness. God muses, "Should I hide from Abraham what I am doing?" (Genesis 18:16) and determines to tell Abraham. The Torah then declares, Abraham stepped forward and said to God, "Will you sweep away the innocent along with the guilty? What if there are fifty innocent people in the city? . . . Far be it from you to do such a thing!" (Genesis 18:23, 25).

Abraham was willing to admonish even God when he sensed that God was going to sin by perverting justice and harming the innocent. Abraham was willing to risk all, step forward and speak truth, even at his own peril, even to God.

Rule No. 4: Love demands that we find a way to intervene.

Love demands that we sometimes must risk all, even the relationship itself, in order to try to help someone we love. The commandment to love your neighbor as yourself means that we must ask ourselves how we ourselves would like to be treated. Do I not truly want others to intervene when I am headed down a harmful path? Rabbi Yossi Bar Hanina (Israel, third century) quoting the book of Proverbs 9:8, "Rebuke a wise man, and he will love you" taught: "Any love that has no rebuke in it is not true love" (*Bereishit Rabba* 54:3).

I want my friends to keep me honest. I don't always like it, but I definitely want it. I am a mass of contradictions, selfish and honorable, petty and noble, and I need help keeping track. I know I need help. I know that creating a holy community, as our *parashah* instructs us, is a road that we will forever be traveling, and that I will lose my way without companions. I welcome their loving guidance, and I will offer mine as well in the name of love.

31

Emor | אמר

An Eye for an Eye?

וְאִישׁ כִּי־יִתֵּן מוּם בַּעֲמִיתוֹ כַּאֲשֶׁר עָשָׂה כֵּן יֵעָשֶׂה לּוֹ: שֶׁבֶר
תַּחַת שֶׁבֶר עַיִן תַּחַת עַיִן שֵׁן תַּחַת שֵׁן כַּאֲשֶׁר יִתֵּן מוּם בָּאָדָם
כֵּן יִנָּתֶן בּוֹ:

*V'ish ki yitein mum ba'amito, ka'asher asah kein
yei'aseh lo: shever takhat shever, ayin takhat ayin,
shein takhat shein. Ka'asher yitein mum ba'adam, kein
yinaten bo.*

A person who inflicts injury on his fellow, as he did so shall be
done to him: a fracture for a fracture, an eye for an eye, a tooth
for a tooth. However he injured his fellow, so shall be done to
him (Leviticus 24:19–20).

"Very good. That way the whole world will be blind and tooth-
less" (Tevye in *Fiddler on the Roof*).[1]

---

1. Joseph Stein, drawing from Sholom Aleichem's Yiddish stories about Tevye the
Dairyman.

TORAH SERVES NOT AS the last word, but as the foundation of Judaism's legal and ethical tradition. This tradition took shape some 3,000 years ago and has evolved continually since that time. I want to remind us of this fact because of the durable stereotype that much Christian thought foists upon the Jews: Judaism is the religion of law, while Christianity is the religion of love. In that telling, when Christianity emerged, Judaism somehow became frozen in time, rejecting the New Testament, forever stranded in the obsolete ancient paradigm of harsh justice that Christianity was here to transcend.

My transformative explorations with wonderful Christian colleagues of the first-century origins of Christianity and Rabbinic Judaism have put to rest that long-standing misconception. The interpretation of Torah and reinvention of Judaism undertaken by the first-century's rabbis (and their predecessors and descendants) line up closely with the teachings of Jesus, himself obviously a first-century Jewish teacher. Jews and Christians are originally "cut from the same cloth." I am encouraged by the rapid spread of this emerging understanding, which undermines the premises of anti-Semitism and provides a fertile common ground for a new kind of relationship between our sibling traditions.

Nonetheless, the stereotype persists. Often, when newcomers to Torah study encounter some of the Torah's harsher pronouncements, they assume that Judaism still stands for these ancient codes, and their prejudices are confirmed. And no text has been used against Judaism more than "an eye for an eye." It is known in Latin as *lex talionis*, "the law of retaliation." *Lex talionis* is repeated elsewhere in the Torah in even more extreme tones and includes not only parts of the body, but life itself: "a life for a life" (Exodus 21:23, Deuteronomy 19:20). These laws are assumed to exemplify a Jewish obsession with strict and retaliatory justice that leaves no room for forgiveness and compassion.

In fact, Rabbinic Judaism openly and emphatically rejects the plain meaning of *lex talionis* in the Torah, and insists that henceforth it stands for compensatory damages—that is, the value of an eye for an eye, or the value of a tooth for a tooth. The Talmud develops a comprehensive set of standards for compensation, taking into account damages, pain, medical expenses, incapacitation and mental anguish, contributing to the foundation of many modern legal codes.

But the rabbis go further in creating the legal and moral foundation for their audacious recasting of the plain meaning of the Torah. They expand another principle of the Torah in order to make the wanton disfiguring or extinguishing of a human being a moral wrong. Genesis 1:27 states, "And God created the human being in the Divine Image; male and female God created them." The rabbis reason that if we are created in the image of God, then disfiguring a person somehow is a "disfigurement" of God as well. Further, if we are made in the image of God and God is infinite, then the value of a human life must also be infinite. There can be no possible compensatory payment for the loss of a human life. Therefore, capital punishment, which is mandated for a variety of transgressions in the Torah, must not be practiced, and with great audacity the rabbis create legislation that makes it virtually impossible for a court to assess the death penalty on a defendant.

The rabbis emphasize the inestimable value of each human life with the indelible phrase, "One who saves a life saves an entire world; one who destroys a life destroys an entire world" (Mishnah Sanhedrin 4:5). This becomes the foundation and the crowning glory of Judaism, leaving the law of retaliation in the ancient past.

As an inheritor of the rabbinic way, Tevye can declare, "As the Good Book says ...," and then disagree with it at the same time. "On the one hand, on the other hand"—our rabbis kept our Torah alive by adapting it, even overruling it. What *chutzpah*!

32 ——————————

Behar | בהר

We Do Not Own the Earth

וְהָאָרֶץ לֹא תִמָּכֵר לִצְמִתֻת כִּי־לִי הָאָרֶץ כִּי־גֵרִים וְתוֹשָׁבִים
אַתֶּם עִמָּדִי:

V'ha'aretz lo timakheir l'tzmitut, ki li ha'aretz, ki geirim v'toshavim atem imadi.

The land cannot be sold in perpetuity, for the land belongs to Me, and you are but temporary residents on My earth (Leviticus 25:23).

DISCUSSING THE PREVIOUS PORTION of *Emor,* I argued for the importance of understanding the expansive evolution that Jewish law and practice have undergone over the centuries. But human history is not a continuous march of progress. While we have advanced in certain understandings of what is good and just, we have regressed in others, and none more so than in our relationship with the earth. Here, the agrarian culture of the Torah has critical lessons to teach us, ancient wisdom that must be reclaimed.

Most central to our modern misconception of our relationship to nature is the idea that we humans can actually own land and the resources beneath that land, as if the earth was only a commodity to be exploited rather than the living matrix from which we ourselves spring. In contrast to this contemporary delusion, Psalm 24 opens, "The earth is the Lord's and all that it contains, the world and all who inhabit it." For our ancestors, everything comes from and belongs to the Creator. We are here by God's grace and owe an incalculable debt for the gift we have received of being able to glean our sustenance from the earth.

Behar lays out the framework by which we might constantly remind ourselves that we are not the masters of creation. Every seventh year, the earth gets a Sabbath. We relinquish our control over the land and let it rest. The land becomes ownerless, and all are free to eat its fruits.

> But in the seventh year, the land shall have a complete rest, a Sabbath of YHVH; you shall not sow your field, nor shall you prune your vineyard. You shall not reap the aftergrowth of your harvest, and you shall not pick the grapes, for it is a year of rest for the land. Whatever the land produces during this Sabbath is available to eat, for you, for the servants in your household, for the hired worker and the foreigner in your household, and for the domestic animals and for the wild beasts that are in your land (Leviticus 25:4–7).

Just as the Torah instructs us that every seventh day is a day of rest for us, and for all the people and animals that work for us, the seventh year is an even broader sabbatical for the entire ecosystem.

The Torah gives a clear rationale for these practices. We are to observe the Sabbath to remember that "YHVH created the heaven and earth and sea and all that is in them" (Exodus 20:11), and to remember "that you were a slave in Egypt, and YHVH your God freed you from there with a mighty hand and an outstretched arm" (Deuteronomy 5:15). That is, by holding to the weekly and yearly Sabbath cycle, we regularly remind ourselves that we owe our lives and our sustenance to the Creator—a corrective against our innate pull to exploit the world for our own benefit. The Torah teaches that, as with Pharaoh, an unchecked lust for control, security and power is in direct conflict with God's plan for an earth and a society in sacred balance. Limitless taking leads ultimately to calamity.

Behar also instructs us to count seven cycles of seven years and explains that after 49 years, the 50th year is the יוֹבֵל *Yoveil*, the Jubilee year.[1] In the Jubilee year, any family that has lost their landholding over the previous years due to debt or misfortune is able to reclaim their land and begin again. This may be the most radical commandment in the Torah: If you are a wealthy landowner, and even if you have come by all of your holdings fair and square, after 50 years you have to give back what you acquired. The Torah explains that you do not actually own that property; you only possess the yield of the land, not the land itself. We are all leaseholders from God. In the Jubilee year, the entire society gets a giant "reset," and both ecological and economic balance are restored. YHVH declares that "the land cannot be sold in perpetuity, for the land belongs to Me, and you are but temporary residents on My earth" (Leviticus 25:23).

The Jubilee is the utopian vision of a society manifesting immense wisdom and fairness. Historically speaking, we cannot verify whether the lofty ideals of the Jubilee year were entirely practiced in ancient Israel. I have difficulty imagining it. But the message and philosophy of the Torah are clear, and represent a sustainable and wise understanding of our right relationship to the natural world, which we ignore at our peril.

Our agrarian and pastoral ancestors knew that they were "just passing through" God's good earth, and needed to steward its resources and live in balance with nature's rhythms. They created legislation to ensure that balance, and along with it enshrined an understanding of our place not as owners, but as residents upon that earth. Today our earth desperately needs a sabbatical, and the consequences of our failures in this regard are becoming terrifyingly real as our climate destabilizes. Global solutions are difficult to achieve, but we have no choice other than to engage this challenge. The Torah can be one of our guides as we nurture a renewed consciousness to care for our Mother Earth.

---

1. *Yoveil* appears to be a synonym for *shofar*, a ram's horn: "You shall proclaim [the 50th year] with shofar blasts on the Day of Atonement; you shall sound the shofar throughout your land" (Leviticus 25:9). In the early Greek and then Latin translations of the Torah, *Yoveil* is rendered as *jubilaeus,* and becomes conflated with another Latin word, *jubilare,* to shout for joy, the source of "jubilation." The English "jubilee" combines these meanings, so that today jubilee means both an anniversary, often the 50th, and also a celebration.

33

Bekhukotai | בחקתי

Fear Itself

וְרָדַף אֹתָם קוֹל עָלֶה נִדָּף . . . וְכָשְׁלוּ אִישׁ־בְּאָחִיו כְּמִפְּנֵי־חֶרֶב
וְרֹדֵף אָיִן

*V'radaf otam kol aleh nidaf . . . V'khashlu ish b'akhiv
k'mipnei kherev v'rodeif ayin*

The mere sound of a wind-driven leaf will put them to flight
. . . even though no one is pursuing them, they will stumble
over one another as if fleeing the sword (Leviticus 26:36–37).

LAST WEEK'S PORTION, *BEHAR*, laid out the need for the earth to receive a sabbatical year every seventh year and our responsibility to let the
land rest. *Bekhukotai*, the final chapters of the book of Leviticus, now describes the consequences of these directives. If we give the land its sabbaths,
we will live in peace and harmony. If we deny the earth its sabbaths, the
outcome will be dire. In terrifying detail, *Bekhukotai* describes a cascade of
misfortune that will befall those who exploit the land without pause. The
land will reject us; it will literally spit us out. We will become homeless and
hounded. We will lose our dignity and self-respect. As our exile reaches its

nadir, we will become so debased that we will be consumed by anxiety and fear: "The mere sound of a wind-driven leaf will put them to flight . . ."

As always, the Torah then offers a message of hope. There will ultimately be return and renewal, another chance for redemption. But the vivid language of fear is what stays with the reader; "even though no one is pursuing them, they will stumble over one another as if fleeing the sword."

Bekhukotai, along with its companion portion *Behar*, offers eerily prescient warnings for our own era of the potentially devastating consequences if humanity is unable to live in sustainable balance with our planet. Will the earth spit us out until "it makes up for the Sabbath years that were denied it"? (Leviticus 26:34). What manner of terrifying consequences are we facing if we fail to find a sustainable rhythm of rest to balance our drive for attainment and consumption?

These questions haunt me as I reflect on the Torah's narrative. But the teaching I want to pursue at this moment is less about our collective fate then about our individual psyches as we each confront the unknown horizon. The Torah describes our very lowest condition as one in which we are driven by fear and anxiety. That is, even more debilitating than being actually terrorized is the state in which we perpetually live in fear, permanently adrenalized, unable to distinguish a real threat from the sound of a leaf blowing in the wind. In this condition, we are unable to manifest that most sublime and central aspect of being a person: the ability to remain aware of our surroundings, assess what our next action might be and then act with volition. To be reduced to anxiety-driven, fight-or-flight reactivity, unable to evaluate what might actually be going on around us, disables our greatest human gift—the ability to think, decide and act.

Some of you may be familiar with the words of Rabbi Nachman of Bratslav (1772–1810) that we sing in my congregation every year at Rosh Hashanah:

כָּל הָעוֹלָם כֻּלּוֹ גֶּשֶׁר צַר מְאֹד וְהָעִיקָר לֹא לְפַחֵד כְּלָל

Kol ha'olam kulo gesher tzar me'od, v'ha'ikar lo l'fakheid klal

"The entire world is a very narrow bridge, and the essential thing is not to fear at all."

The message is noble and inspiring. The melody was composed in Israel by Rabbi Baruch Chait during the 1973 Yom Kippur War. If there was ever a moment that called for Jews to cross that narrow bridge fearlessly, it was at that terrifying moment when Israel's life hung in the balance.

Yet many have pointed out that the instruction to "not fear at all" is unrealistic. Truly, courage is the ability to act despite one's fears. When standing on the cusp of important decisions, even decisions that are not life-threatening, who is not afraid? The artist Georgia O'Keeffe famously said, "I've been absolutely terrified every moment of my life—and I've never let it keep me from doing a single thing I wanted to do." So maybe Reb Nachman's instruction needs to be more nuanced.

And, in fact, Reb Nachman's original statement is more nuanced. Baruch Chait created an eminently singable lyric, but as I learned from Rabbi Aura Ahuvia, he did so by simplifying Reb Nachman's original words. Reb Nachman taught:

וְדַע, שֶׁהָאָדָם צָרִיךְ לַעֲבֹר עַל גֶּשֶׁר צַר מְאֹד מְאֹד וְהַכְּלָל וְהָעִקָּר שֶׁלֹּא יִתְפַּחֵד כְּלָל

V'da, she'ha'adam tzarikh la'avor al gesher tzar me'od me'od, v'ha'klal v'ha'ikar—she'lo yitpakheid klal.

And know, that a human being must cross over a very, very narrow bridge, and it is critically important that he *not fill himself with fear* (Likutei Tinyana 48, italics mine).

Ah, the difference a verb construct can make! לְפַחֵד *L'fakhed* means "to fear"; לְהִתְפַּחֵד *l'hitpakhed* means "to cause oneself to fear." Reb Nachman was not telling us not to fear. Reb Nachman was telling us that despite life being full of potential dangers, don't freak yourself out! Indeed, life is challenging enough without us working ourselves into a lather of anxiety about what might happen next. Filling oneself with fear does not help; it actually makes us less able to navigate the narrow bridge. The challenge we all face is to remain aware of our anxieties, but not allow them to rule us. We must work on distinguishing between external risks and internal anxieties. Fear makes us rigid. Balancing across the narrow bridge of life requires supple steps. There is no guarantee that we will not fall. There are no guarantees! But rigidity inevitably makes us less able to make the subtle shifts of weight and direction that allow us to remain upright as we traverse the tightrope of our lives.

Indeed, at the beginning of *Bekhukotai*, as God describes the blessings that will accrue to us if we live in balance with the land, God says "I, YHVH, am your God who brought you out of the Land of Egypt to be slaves no more, who broke the bars of your yoke so that you could walk erect" (Leviticus 26:13). I see this erect posture, this liberation from the oppressive terror of slavery, as the direct contrast to the debased condition in which we will once again find ourselves if we lose our balance and succumb to fear, falling over one another in flight even though no one pursues us. True freedom includes the inner capacity to distinguish between real and imagined dangers; rather than cower or flee or lash out indiscriminately, we need to be able to assess our fears and walk upright on our paths.

We move on now to סֵפֶר בְּמִדְבָּר *Sefer Bamidbar,* the book of Numbers. If only the Children of Israel were indeed ready to walk upright, instead of constantly being bowed and driven by their fears. But alas, these former slaves have many painful lessons ahead of them as they make their circuitous way from fear to faith.

במדבר
Numbers

כן יהיה תמיד הענן יכסנו ומראה־אש לילה

And so it was always: a cloud covered [by day] and an
appearance of fire at night. (Numbers 9:16)

34 ———————————————

Bamidbar | במדבר

In the Wilderness

וַיְדַבֵּ֨ר יְהֹוָ֧ה אֶל־מֹשֶׁ֛ה בְּמִדְבַּ֥ר סִינַ֖י בְּאֹ֣הֶל מוֹעֵ֑ד בְּאֶחָד֩ לַחֹ֨דֶשׁ
הַשֵּׁנִ֜י בַּשָּׁנָ֣ה הַשֵּׁנִ֗ית לְצֵאתָ֛ם מֵאֶ֥רֶץ מִצְרַ֖יִם

*Va'yedabeir YHVH el Moshe b'Midbar Sinai b'ohel
mo'eid b'ekhad la'khodesh ha'sheini bashanah
ha'sheinit l'tzeitam mei'eretz Mitzrayim*

YHVH spoke to Moses in the Wilderness of Sinai in the Tent
of Meeting on the first day of the second month of the second
year since leaving Egypt (Numbers 1:1).

So BEGINS THE FOURTH book of the Torah. Its English name is the
book of Numbers, from the Greek *Arithmoi*, based on the elaborate census
takings that make up several of the book's chapters. But the Hebrew name
is *Bamidbar*, which means "In the Wilderness." It is a much more descriptive title, as the entire narrative takes place in a series of wilderness regions
stretching from the Sinai Peninsula up through the present-day Negev, and
into the mountains and plains of Edom and Moab on the Eastern bank
of the Jordan River, covering the last 39 of the 40 years of the Israelites'
tumultuous wanderings.

Our sages engineered the cycle of Torah readings so that this first portion of the book, also titled *Bamidbar*, would always fall on the Shabbat just prior to the Festival of Shavuot. Shavuot is the festival that marks our receiving of the Torah at Mount Sinai. Why did the sages intentionally connect this portion *Bamidbar* with the receiving of Torah?

Our sages are very clear that the Torah had to be given in the wilderness. The wilderness is land that belongs to no one. It is untracked; undomesticated. In order to hear the voice of God, we must find a way to clear our minds of the details and involvements of our daily lives. We also must, at least for a time, give up some measure of control of our lives and encounter life without preconditions. One way to do this is by heading out into the wilderness. I am an avid hiker, and I know well the restorative nature of spending time wandering in the wild. My thoughts gradually slow down and the din of my inner preoccupations diminishes until I am able to hear the world wordlessly speaking to me. I inevitably return to my very mapped-out life feeling clearer and renewed. *Sh'ma*, "listen." It makes perfect sense that our ancestors would see the wilderness as the place to go to hear the voice of God.

But shifting our location in space is not the only way to create a "wilderness area." If we can give up our ownership and domestication of time—that is, carve out holy time in which we pause from our work—then we can create a "wild" zone in time in which our busy minds might be stilled so that we might hear God's voice. This is, of course, the idea of Shabbat and Holy Days. Even a relationship can at times become a blessed wandering in the wilderness if we are able even for a moment to set aside our expectations and opinions about the other person, and instead wander into the great mystery of their eyes and breath and the burning bush of their shimmering presence.

The Hebrew name for wilderness, מִדְבָּר *midbar*, draws us even deeper into this understanding. In Hebrew grammar, if you take a verb and place the prefix mi- before it, the resulting word means, "the place where that activity happens." For example, the verbal root שׁ־כ־נ SH-K-N means "dwell," and מִשְׁכַּן MiSHKaN means "dwelling place," and in the Torah is the term for the sanctuary where God's presence dwells. ק־ד־שׁ K-D-SH means "sanctify" or "holy," and מִקְדָּשׁ MiKDaSH is the "place of holiness," and the בֵּית הַמִּקְדָּשׁ *Beit Hamikdash* is the Hebrew term for the ancient holy sanctuary in Jerusalem. In a more mundane vein, ט־ב־ח TaBaKH means "cook"; מִטְבָּח MiTBaKH is a kitchen.

With this grammatical form in mind, *midbar* reveals a curious etymology: ד–ב–ר D-B-R means "speak." מִדְבָּר MiDBaR therefore must mean "the place of speech," or perhaps "the place of speaking." Does that mean that our ancestors understood the wilderness as the place we go to hear God speak with us? I can't prove it, but it seems right to me. The place or state of consciousness in which we might hear God's voice is the place we do not control, the place we try to leave undisturbed by our ambitions, the place where we are humbled by creation's grandeur, the place we do not try to domesticate with our comfortable categories. It can be a terrifying place because at least for a time, we leave our comforts and our shelter behind, and walk vulnerably into the unknown. This is where the Great Mystery speaks to us, and this is where the deeper meaning of life is wordlessly revealed. Our tradition teaches that even though the Children of Israel all heard that Voice together when they stood at Mount Sinai—the moment we celebrate and hope to recreate as we celebrate Shavuot—that Voice has never ceased. It was, is and will be always reverberating through our parched souls. Our challenge is to make the time and space in our lives to venture out into the *midbar* and listen.

35

Naso | נשא

Be a Channel for Blessings

יְבָרֶכְךָ יְהֹוָה וְיִשְׁמְרֶךָ:

Yevarekhekha Adonai v'yishmerekha.

May the Source of Life bless you and protect you (Numbers 6:24).

THE MOST ANCIENT JEWISH prayer that we still know and recite today appears in this week's Torah portion. It is known as בִּרְכַּת כֹּהֲנִים *Birkat Kohanim*—the Priestly Blessing and also as בִּרְכַּת הַשָּׁלוֹם *Birkat Hashalom*—The Blessing of Peace:

> YHVH spoke to Moses, saying: speak to Aaron and his sons and tell them how to bless the Children of Israel. They shall say:
> May YHVH bless you and protect you.
> May YHVH fill you with light and grace.
> May YHVH's countenance be lifted towards you and fill you with peace.
> In this way, you will link my Ineffable Name to the Children of Israel, and I will be blessing them (Numbers 6:22–27).

The instructions are clear: Aaron and his sons are to be conduits so that Divine energy and goodness can flow into the Children of Israel.

In Jewish mystical thought, the direct energy of God is too great for a body to bear. The unmediated light of God is compared to the light and heat of the sun. The sun's light and heat sustain us, but the light is too strong to stare at directly and too much of its heat will burn us. A modern analogy is that of electricity. The direct current from the power plant will fry all of our appliances—transformers are required to reduce the current, sometimes down to a trickle, so that it runs our motors or charges our batteries without blowing them up. This is one way that the earlier deaths of Aaron's sons Nadav and Avihu (Leviticus 10:1–2) are explained: When they entered the sanctuary illicitly, they were not prepared to be conduits of the great energy of life, creativity and consciousness that is God. It was more than their systems could bear.

Our mystics hold that because the Creator wants us to live, the immense and potentially destructive energy that fuels the universe is transformed and reduced, like the sun's rays, so that it sustains our lives rather than destroys them.

As partners in creation, we humans are assigned the task of being conduits and transformers of this Divine energy. This is our holy challenge. We can curse as well as bless, destroy as well as create. Being a conduit for blessing requires caring attention and constant choice. I hope to take the life energy that flows through me and transform it as skillfully and lovingly as I can so that what emerges from me is a source of blessing, encouragement and inspiration to others. Through my words and actions, I want to be a vehicle for creativity, life and goodness. It's a wonderful skill to practice, like practicing a musical instrument until you can reliably produce beautiful sounds with it. Like most of us, I have a lot of work to do until I'm really good at being a channel for blessing.

There is a beautiful incentive for choosing to offer blessing instead of curse or choosing blessing instead of indifference. When we offer blessing to another person—and this can be as simple as wishing them well, no fancy words needed—we, too, are blessed. We are blessed by the connection we make to another, and we are especially blessed by the very energy that flows through us in the act of blessing.

When we think of ourselves as channels, we will never run dry. The blessing is not coming from us; it is coming *through* us. We are simply allowing the energy of life and the bounty of goodness that we are continually receiving from the Source of All to move through us; what greater goodness could we want or expect?

May we use our intelligence, love and awareness to shape, direct and articulate that energy so that when we encounter someone in need of a blessing at that moment in their life, precisely the right and needed words or gestures emerge from our beings. May we be generous with our blessings, knowing that they flow from an inexhaustible source. And may every muscle, cell and fiber of our own being vibrate and be saturated with the goodness that flows through us when we bless.

36

Beha'alotekha | בהעלתך

Are We There Yet?

וַיְהִי הָעָם כְּמִתְאֹנְנִים רַע בְּאָזְנֵי יְהוָֹה

Va'yehi ha'am k'mit'onanim ra b'oznei YHVH

The people took to complaining bitterly before YHVH
(Numbers 11:1).

AFTER MORE THAN A year encamped at Mount Sinai, the time has come
for the Children of Israel to march to the Promised Land. Transformed
from a throng of refugee slaves, they are now organized into tribes and
troops, bound by laws, a newly covenanted community. Their task is to
follow the protecting Cloud of the Divine Presence. The Cloud lifts, the
Children of Israel break camp, and they follow the cloud on a three-day
journey.

And then, they begin complaining. This week's *parashah,* along with
the following three *parashiyot,* vividly describe a series of escalating complaints, betrayals and outright rebellions by the Children of Israel against
Moses and YHVH. The outcome of this recalcitrance is catastrophic: Instead of entering the Promised Land, the Children of Israel are condemned
to 40 years of homeless wandering.

There is nothing dry about these portions. They are filled with high drama, pathos and also humor, and they resonate on every level of experience.

On one level, this is the story of a family. The Children of Israel are literally the children, and Moses and YHVH are the parents. The children are impulsive. They continually fall apart. They fight. They complain. They say they will follow the commandments, then they forget, then they make excuses. I often think of them in the back of the minivan, while YHVH and Moses take turns driving on a road trip that feels endless from the constant whining and bellowing from the rear of the car . . . Moses and YHVH alternate losing their tempers, threatening consequences and calming each other down. Are we there yet?

The journey through the wilderness is a crucible in which the children must grow up. The certainties, constraints and lack of responsibility of Egypt are gone, and they are being forced to enter into adult relationship with the world and with each other. They must learn to control their impulses, delay gratification, and learn empathy and trust. The journey is not straightforward. It wanders—three steps forward, two steps back. And Moses and YHVH, out of their love for their children, hang in there, and continue to forgive the kids and give them another chance.

In one of my favorite passages in this chapter, completely undone by the complaining, Moses speaks to God out of a frustration that every parent probably recognizes:

> "What have you done to me? . . . Am I supposed to carry this people on my bosom like a nursing mother all the way to the Promised Land? . . . I can't do it. If this is the way it is going to be, just kill me now!" (Numbers 11:11–15).

YHVH responds with a promise to expand Moses's leadership circle (or, we might say, make sure there is more childcare available). In addition to a family saga, *Beha'alotekha* and the succeeding portions are also about political leadership.[1] From where does Moses draw his authority? What makes him a leader? How can he carry the burden of leadership by himself? YHVH tells Moses to gather 70 elders and "bring them to the Tent of Meeting, and let them take their place there with you . . . and I will draw upon the spirit that is in you and put it on them; they shall share the burden of the people with you, and you shall not bear it alone" (Numbers 11:16–17).

1. See, for example, *Moses as Political Leader* by Aaron Wildavsky, Shalem Press, 2005.

All is going well, the spirit rests on the elders, and they begin to speak in ecstasy, filled with the word of God. But two others, Eldad and Medad, who are not in the Tent of Meeting but rather back in the camp, also begin to prophesy! This is not authorized; Joshua, distressed, tells Moses to stop them. Moses famously replies: "Are you distressed on my account? Would that all of God's people were prophets, and that the spirit rested on all of them!" (Numbers 11:29).

Here, we witness Moses as a model of political leadership at its best. He is a true public servant. He does not wish to hoard power or elevate himself above the people he serves. His only wish is that everyone would be so imbued with the spirit of leadership that Moses himself would not need to wield that authority over others.

Nonetheless, his brother and sister, Miriam and Aaron, immediately challenge Moses again: "Has YHVH spoken only through Moses? Has YHVH not spoken through us as well?" (Numbers 12:2). God afflicts Miriam for her challenge, and Moses responds by praying for her healing. Despite his bouts of frustration and despair, and episodes in which he powerfully asserts his authority to quell rebellion, Moses always has his heart with his people. He always keeps his eye on the prize of creating a "nation of priests, a holy people" (Exodus 19:6), a description that could be rephrased as "a society based upon justice, fairness and human dignity."

Finally, this story is about each of us on our own spiritual journey. We are the Children of Israel. We sense there is a better way, a way of trust, a Promised Land to which we aspire to merit and to inhabit. Yet our commitment to this path is constantly impeded by our own resistance, our own pettiness, our own learned powerlessness. The path forward is hard, with no certainties or guarantees. We romanticize the past (Egypt?), and wish to abdicate from the present and from the future. We complain, we cower, we want to bolt. We know that we often seem ludicrous, even pathetic, but we also often can't help it. Let's have some compassion for ourselves and keep a sense of humor! However, in order to pursue our destinies, we have to confront all of these failings. We must stand upright, face the unknown and trust that the manna will be there to sustain us, and that the Cloud is leading us in a worthy direction even though we have never been there before. This battle rages within every single human heart every day: Leave Egypt behind, despite the certainty it gave you in your smallness. Choose trust over fear, choose agency over paralysis, choose courage over cowardice. Choose life.

Fortunately, each of us not only is an Israelite; we are all also Moses. That voice resides within us as well. That voice knows that going back to Egypt is not our destiny. That voice cajoles and encourages, demands and nags: You can do this! You can take the next step. You can learn from your mistakes. You can grow in wisdom, no matter what your chronological age. Every moment, this very moment, is an opportunity to look up from your preoccupations and see where the Cloud of the Presence is leading you next on this great and unpredictable journey.

37

Shelakh | שלח

Healing the Crushed Spirit

וַנְּהִי בְעֵינֵינוּ כַּחֲגָבִים וְכֵן הָיִינוּ בְּעֵינֵיהֶם:

Va'nehi v'eineinu kakhagavim, v'khein hayinu b'eineihem.

We looked like grasshoppers to ourselves, so we certainly must have looked that way to them (Numbers 13:33).

THE CHILDREN OF ISRAEL are preparing to enter the Promised Land. Moses sends 12 scouts, one from each tribe, to explore this land they had heard flowed with milk and honey. Forty days later, the scouts return. They bring back evidence of the land's fruitfulness—an enormous cluster of grapes. But then 10 of the scouts offer a damning report: The inhabitants are enormous Titans. They will devour us. Another scout, Caleb, vigorously disputes their assessment: "We must, we must go up to the land and take possession of it, for we surely, surely can do it" (Numbers 13:30). But the 10 then deliver their coup de grace: "We looked like grasshoppers to ourselves, so we certainly must have looked that way to them" (Numbers 13:33). Certain defeat awaits.

145

At this, the entire community bursts into wails and weeps through the night: "We're going to die! If only we had died in Egypt! Let's turn around and head back to Egypt!" (Numbers 14:2, 4). Total bedlam ensues.

As a result of this collective nervous breakdown, YHVH declares that the people are not ready to enter the Promised Land. They will instead wander for 40 years until the slave generation has passed away and a new generation raised in freedom comes of age. Of the generation that left Egypt, only Caleb and Joshua, who were among the 12 scouts and who were the only ones who believed that the Children of Israel could attain their goal, would live to see the Promised Land.

The moral of this tale is clear: If you think of yourself as a lowly insect, you are unlikely to attain your goals. But if, additionally, you are convinced that *everyone else* thinks you are an insect, then you are certain to fail. You are unlikely to even try. You might as well head back to Egypt, the place where crushed spirits dwell.

So many of us were conditioned or even abused as children; we concluded that we were less worthy, intelligent or deserving of a place in the sun than most everyone around us. So many of us learned to enter a new social situation in fear, assuming that we were somehow uniquely unwelcome. This is certainly the adolescent nightmare that almost everyone I know once faced or faces today. That sense of smallness is disabling in and of itself. But then we compound our insecurity by projecting our own self-judgments onto the people around us: "I'm sure no one wants to hear what I have to say. After all, it is obvious to everyone how unimportant I am."

Says who? How did we get this damning idea in our heads? Why do we do this to ourselves? Are we not all children of God?

In Chapter 6 of Exodus, Moses makes a stirring speech to the Israelite slaves, promising that YHVH has heard their cries, and that their liberation is coming. "But the people would not listen to Moses, their spirits crushed by cruel bondage" (Exodus 6:9). In *Shelakh*, the Israelites have left slavery, but has the crushing imprint of slavery left them? This is the lifelong challenge we each face: to contest our "learned powerlessness"; to recondition ourselves, day by day, to think of ourselves and to act as fundamentally equal to and worthy as those around us. Only then will the Promised Land appear attainable to our eyes.

Let's practice together. Assuming that most of us are still feeling like grasshoppers a certain amount of the time, let's remind one another with encouraging demeanor and words that, however lowly you may think of yourself, your projection that we share the same low opinion of you is unfounded, even ridiculous. As we worship the Power in the Universe that liberates the slave, let us serve that Power and work to heal one another's crushed spirit.

In Leviticus 26:13, YHVH declares: "I, Life Unfolding, am your God who brought you out from Egypt to be slaves no more, who broke the bars of your yoke so that you might walk erect." As with the slaves in Egypt, the first and necessary step is to liberate the oppressed and the abused from the yoke of cruel oppression. But that is only the beginning. We must also help liberate one another from the yoke of a crushed spirit, so that we might feel cared for and confident enough to straighten our backs and walk upright together towards our Promised Land.

Ken y'hi ratzon—So may it be.

38 ———————————

Korakh | קרח

Demagogue

וַיִּקָּהֲלוּ עַל־מֹשֶׁה וְעַל־אַהֲרֹן וַיֹּאמְרוּ אֲלֵהֶם רַב־לָכֶם כִּי כָל־
הָעֵדָה כֻּלָּם קְדֹשִׁים וּבְתוֹכָם יְהוָה וּמַדּוּעַ תִּתְנַשְּׂאוּ עַל־קְהַל
יְהוָה:

Vayik'halu al Moshe v'al Aharon vayomru aleihem:
"Rav lakhem, ki khol ha'eidah kulam kedoshim
u'v'tokham YHVH—u'madua titnas'u al k'hal
YHVH?"

And [Korakh and his followers] gathered against Moses and
Aaron and said to them, "You have gone too far! Is not the
entire community holy, and is not YHVH in their midst? Why
do you raise yourselves up above the community?!" (Numbers
16:3).

Demagogue: a political leader who seeks support by appeal-
ing to popular desires and prejudices rather than by using
rational argument (*Merriam-Webster*).

148

KORAKH ASSEMBLES 250 ISRAELITE leaders and publicly confronts Moses and Aaron: "Why do you merit to be the leaders?" Korakh's argument sounds reasonable—did not YHVH speak to all of the Children of Israel at Mount Sinai? Did they not all enter into covenant with YHVH at the mountain? Does not the Divine Presence dwell among all of them? Why then should the brothers Moses and Aaron have the power of Chief Judge and High Priest? How about a little more power-sharing here? And did not Moses himself recently exclaim, "Would that all YHVH's people were prophets!" (Numbers 13:29).

It sounds good, but the sages and Jewish tradition don't buy it. Instead, the sages examine what can be learned about Korakh elsewhere in the Torah, and determine that his words are hollow and self-serving. They then read between the lines and *midrashically* paint Korakh as the embodiment of demagoguery, a phenomenon they clearly are deeply acquainted with (when it comes to human behavior, there is nothing new under the sun), and they hold Korakh up as the exemplar of this form of dangerous political leadership.

The commentators note that Korakh is not an ordinary citizen. He is Moses's and Aaron's first cousin. He is part of the priestly elite, and his role is to care for and transport the Ark of the Covenant and all the other sacred objects that furnish the Holy of Holies. Korakh is clearly among the most privileged Israelites. The *midrash* describes Korakh as exceedingly wealthy as well.

Just prior to the verse cited at the beginning of this essay, *Parashat Korakh* opens with an unusual wording: וַיִּקַּח קֹרַח *Vayikakh Korakh* . . . —"And Korakh took . . ." (16:1). Took what? Why does the Torah not say, "And Korakh arose" or "And Korakh gathered around himself . . ." The *midrash* expands upon this strange opening and explains: Korakh took people in with words. His followers were taken in by Korakh's rhetoric. Korakh, the rabbis assert, possesses the gift of gab. He knows how to inflame his followers' grievances and reinforce their sense of entitlement. He distorts and selectively ignores the truth in order to win people over.

For example, the other named leaders that Korakh gathers around him have their own reasons to be aggrieved at their exclusion from the highest echelons. Datan, Aviram and On are all of the tribe of Reuben. If you will recall, Reuben was Jacob's firstborn. Yet descendants of the tribe of Levi are in control. Doesn't the Torah explicitly direct the inheritance to go to the firstborn son? Shouldn't they be in charge?

But their emotion ignores history. Their patriarch Reuben long ago fell from grace after he slept with Bilhah, one of his father Jacob's wives. Jacob stripped him of his firstborn privileges (see Genesis 49:3). Yet perhaps Korakh knew just what to say to appeal to the Reubenites' humiliation, to promise them restored status and to get them to stand by his side.

Datan and Aviram themselves are good matches for Korakh when it comes to political theater and twisted rhetoric. When Moses suggests that they and Korakh meet with him to discuss their grievances, Datan and Aviram refuse and call a press conference (as it were), announcing, "We will not come! Is it not enough that you brought us from a land flowing with milk and honey to have us die in the wilderness, that you would also lord it over us?" (Numbers 16:12–13). Datan and Aviram have the temerity to refer to the Israelites' former land of enslavement with the very same language that Moses promises for their future: a land flowing with milk and honey! Ah, claims the populist, remember the good old days . . . how good you all had it then?

The *midrash* further elaborates on Korakh's casuistry (specious argument), creating passages in which he picks apart Moses's instructions and laws, making them seem pointless and burdensome. He proclaims Moses's choice of Aaron as High Priest to be pure nepotism, a brazen attempt to consolidate all the wealth of the priestly tithes in Moses's own family. Korakh incites the people, commenting on how well-fed these leaders appear to be.

As always, the demagogue mines a kernel of truth, which is what gives his argument momentum. Moses does possess great authority; Aaron does receive the best cuts of meat. They are privileged. But Korakh also ignores the greater truth: Moses has never governed for his own enrichment. He carries the burden of leadership without fanfare, just as his brother Aaron carries the sins of the entire People on his shoulders when he seeks God's forgiveness. Aaron and Moses serve a higher purpose and resist the aggrandizing temptations of power. But Korakh, despite his compelling rhetoric and his populist appeals, serves no one but himself.

Thus, Jewish tradition uses the contrast of Korakh and Moses as an object lesson in leadership, teaching us to be wary of self-serving leaders. In *Pirkei Avot, The Teachings of the Sages,* Korakh becomes immortalized as the example of the wrong path: "Any dispute that is in service of the common good will have enduring value. A dispute that is not in service of the common good has no lasting value. . . . And what is an example of a dispute that has no lasting value? The dispute of Korakh and his companions" (Pirkei Avot 5:17).

In our portion, we are rewarded with a satisfyingly fantastic and wish-fulfilling ending to Korakh's rebellion: The earth opens its mouth and swallows him up along with his cohort. Problem solved, I suppose! But we don't get to expect any miracles in our own political dramas. Rather, we have to remain vigilant against the Korakhs of our day. We must shun the fleeting satisfactions of self-righteous rage that cloud our own good judgment and hone our abilities to argue with reason, and to work with passion for the common good.

39 ——————————————————

Hukat | חקת
Confronting Mortality

וַיָּבֹאוּ בְנֵי־יִשְׂרָאֵל כָּל־הָעֵדָה מִדְבַּר־צִן בַּחֹדֶשׁ הָרִאשׁוֹן וַיֵּשֶׁב
הָעָם בְּקָדֵשׁ וַתָּמָת שָׁם מִרְיָם וַתִּקָּבֵר שָׁם: וְלֹא־הָיָה מַיִם
לָעֵדָה

*Va'yavo'u B'nei Yisrael kol ha'eidah Midbar Tzin
bakhodesh harishon va'yeishev ha'am b'Kadeish.
Vatamot sham Miriam vatikaveir sham. V'lo hayah
mayim la'eidah*

And all the Children of Israel arrived at the Wilderness of
Tzin on the first new moon, and stayed at Kadesh. Miriam
died there and was buried there. And there was no water for
the community (Numbers 20:1–2).

THIRTY-NINE YEARS HAVE PASSED since Moses, Miriam and Aaron
led the Children of Israel out of bondage. Thirty-nine years since Moses
raised his staff and split the sea, and since Miriam led all the women in
dancing on the far shore. Now, Miriam dies.

Aaron will also pass away later in our portion. And Moses will learn
that he, too, will not enter the Promised Land. A generation is passing. Are

the Children of Israel finally ready to "grow up" and find a new generation of leaders?

The Torah tells us that immediately after Miriam's death, the community's water dries up. Miriam's link with water is noted by Jewish tradition. It goes back to her protecting her baby brother Moses as his basket floated down the Nile, and continues with her singing and dancing at the edge of the sea. Miriam becomes known as the keeper of Miriam's Well—a miraculous water source summoned by Miriam that travels with the Israelites through the Wilderness. Now that Miriam is gone, the well dries up. God tells Moses to take his staff and tell the rock to yield its water so that the people might drink.

In one of the more perplexing moments in the Torah, instead of speaking to the rock, Moses shouts at the assembled community: שִׁמְעוּ־נָא הַמֹּרִים הֲמִן־הַסֶּלַע הַזֶּה נוֹצִיא לָכֶם מָיִם *Shim'u na, ha'morim! Ha'min ha'sela ha'zeh notzi lakhem mayim?*—"Listen up, you rebels! Can we get water for you out of this rock?" (Numbers 20:10). Moses then strikes the rock with his staff, and water gushes forth.

But there is no celebration. Instead, YHVH says to Aaron and Moses, "Because you did not trust me enough to affirm my sanctity in front of the Israelites, you shall not lead this people into the Promised Land" (20:12). Is this not too harsh? After a lifetime of selfless leadership, Moses lapses once and is thus condemned to never reach his goal? Readers of all eras are troubled and puzzle over God's decree. How could Moses possibly deserve this fate? I find the many efforts to justify God's decree to be forced and unsatisfying; on the surface, the punishment simply does not fit the transgression. I am much more drawn to a more subtle reading of the text—"a story beneath the story," as Rabbi Jonathan Sacks puts it, that we find encoded in so much of the Torah.

Miriam has just died, and a very human Moses is beside himself with grief. His big sister has protected him since birth. Moses never led alone; he always had his sister and his brother by his side. And now, Miriam is gone, and the water of life has stopped flowing. An all-too-human Moses lashes out in anguish and despair. This is a story about mortality and grief.

In this telling, read "God" as "Life," proclaiming not a punishment, but instead describing reality: "And Life said to Moses, indeed, Miriam is gone, and your time too is soon coming to an end. You will not live to see your most cherished goal. This is the way of Life. It is time to pass the mantle to the next generation."

In this telling, read the odd Hebrew usage with care: when Moses exclaims, *Shim'u na*, הַמֹּרִים *ha'morim!*—"Listen up, you rebels!—HaMoRIM certainly appears to mean "rebels." But this is the only time in Torah that this usage is found. Note that in the unvocalized Hebrew of the Torah, this word could just as easily be read as הַמִּרְיָם HaMiRIaM, thereby rendering the verse as "Hear me, please, Miriam! How are we going to get water out of this rock for these people?"

In the story beneath the story, Moses cries out to his sister. The fact is, Moses knows how to get water from the rock; he accomplished the same task back in Exodus 17:5–6. Something else is going on here: Miriam has just died, and Moses at this moment is utterly bereft. In the aftermath, Moses realizes that he will not be able to complete this journey without his sister. His time is also approaching. There is a time to be born and a time to die, a time for every purpose under heaven.

Aaron is then informed that it is his time to die, and Moses escorts his brother to the peak of Mount Hor. Aaron dies on the summit, and the people mourn. Now only Moses is left of that triumvirate of siblings, and as the Israelites journey onward, it is imperative that they learn how to summon the waters of life into their midst. Life must go on. They arrive at a place simply called "The Well," and there they sing a song to the well . . . and the waters appear!

In this telling, a close reading of the Hebrew is again key: אָז יָשִׁיר יִשְׂרָאֵל אֶת־הַשִּׁירָה הַזֹּאת *Az yashir Yisrael et hashirah ha'zot*—"Then Israel sang this song" (Numbers 21:17) is the very same phrasing, with a key difference, as the song of liberation at the Sea of Reeds: אָז יָשִׁיר־מֹשֶׁה וּבְנֵי יִשְׂרָאֵל אֶת־הַשִּׁירָה הַזֹּאת *Az yashir Moshe uv'nei Yisrael et hashirah ha'zot*—"Then Moses and the Children of Israel sang this song" (Exodus 15:1). Nearly 40 years later, the Children of Israel are now called simply Israel, no longer children, and are singing without Moses!

And what do they sing? עֲלִי בְאֵר עֱנוּ־לָהּ *Ali v'eir, enu la!*—"Spring up, Well—Sing to it!" (Numbers 21:17), reminiscent of the celebration with drums and dance that Miriam led the women in after crossing the sea. But there it says וַתַּעַן לָהֶם מִרְיָם *Va'ta'an la'hem Miriam*—"And Miriam sang to them" (Exodus 15:21). Now, Miriam is no more, and it is the people themselves who are singing, and the waters now flow for them.

In this telling, mortality is confronted, grief is expressed and acknowledged, and life is affirmed. In this telling, the story is about our own journey through life. The waters that dry up when we lose a loved one are not forever lost; we each face the challenge of having to resume the song of life on our own, despite the fact that the loved one who taught us the song, who sang with us and whose loving presence we drank from, is no longer singing. We must journey through our grief, through our own desiccated wilderness, until we can return to the well, and then we must allow to rise within ourselves the song that others used to lead for us. In this telling, after our beloved teachers and parents are gone, it is up to us to become the singers who summon and keep the waters of life flowing for the next generation.

Parashat Hukat begins with an entire chapter about the arcane ritual of the red heifer. The red heifer's ashes, when properly prepared, are to be used in a ritual to restore to wholeness those who have come in contact with the dead. On the surface, these instructions seem obscure, oddly inserted into the narrative that follows. But in the story beneath the story, the connection becomes obvious. The ashes of the red heifer bring us back from the limbo of grief and death, and restore us to the community of the living. This chapter serves as a prelude for our portion. In the next passages, Miriam and Aaron die; Moses encounters his own disabling grief and confronts his own mortality; and the Children of Israel must finally grow up and restore their own sense of wholeness, knowing that death is a part of life. *Hukat* teaches us how to keep singing.

40

Balak | בלק

Mah Tovu—How Good It Is

מַה־טֹבוּ אֹהָלֶיךָ יַעֲקֹב מִשְׁכְּנֹתֶיךָ יִשְׂרָאֵל:

Mah tovu ohalekha Ya'akov, mishkenotekha Yisrael.

How goodly are your tents, Jacob, your dwelling places, Israel
(Numbers 24:5).

THE ISRAELITES ARE JOURNEYING towards the Jordan River and pass
through the territory of King Balak of Moab. Balak is terrified and hires
the prophet Balaam to lay a curse upon the Israelites. Three times Balaam
climbs up to a promontory from which he can survey the Israelite encampment. Each time, instead of a curse, only words of blessing issue from his
lips. King Balak is furious, of course, and reprimands Balaam. But Balaam
reminds him that as a prophet, he is only capable of uttering the words that
God puts in his mouth.

On the final attempt, as Balaam gazes from the highest peak out on a
veritable sea of Israelite tents, he utters: *Mah tovu ohalekha Ya'akov, mishkenotekha Yisrael*—"How goodly are your tents, Jacob, your dwelling places,
Israel!" Our sages plucked this phrase from the Torah and placed it at the
beginning of our morning prayers.

156

Missing from our prayer book, however, is the continuation of Balaam's blessing. In fact, an appropriate translation of *Mah Tovu* is more likely in the form of a question; here is the entire passage, opening with a question and then answering:

> How goodly are your tents, Jacob,
> Your dwelling places, Israel?
> Like palm groves that stretch out,
> Like gardens beside a river,
> Like aloes planted by YHVH,
> Like cedars beside the water,
> Their boughs dripping with moisture,
> Their roots have abundant water (Numbers 24:5–7).

I feel so refreshed by this imagery. I am drawn into an oasis of water and shade. And as I recall the arid and forbidding landscape of the steppes of Moab where the Israelites are camped, the picture that Balaam's words paint becomes even more enticing.

Our sages who placed this verse at the opening of the *siddur*—the prayer book—understood that the purpose of communal prayer is to refresh our spirits. They also assumed that by flagging the first verse of the passage, "How goodly are your tents," the worshippers, knowing their Scripture, would know and think of the verdant description that follows. Life easily becomes a slog through the wilderness, depleting us and distracting us, sucking us dry, so that we forget how good it is to be alive. The purpose of prayer, the purpose of Shabbat, the purpose of entering a synagogue sanctuary (or any other place that feels like a restorative oasis to you) is to ask the question, "How good is it?" and then to list all the ways in which it is truly a blessing to be alive.

This activity does not ignore or negate the difficulties that we face. Rather, it grounds us, refreshes us and fortifies us so that we might not wilt in the heat of our struggles.

We are certainly traveling through frightening and distressing times. But it is also true that life is good, and that we are each immeasurably blessed, and if we can regularly focus on the goodness that sustains us, we will be better able to stay sane and kind and strong as we face the uncertain path ahead. The world needs us—our loved ones and our communities need us—but what do we have left to give if we are dried up and distracted? I hope you can find a community that gathers on Shabbat or some other holy time for the purpose of creating such an oasis together. May you sit in each other's healing shade, drink life in deeply and help each other remember that, with all its challenges, life is good.

41

Pinkhas | פינחס

The Daughters of Tz'lofkhad Step Forward

וַתִּקְרַבְנָה בְּנוֹת צְלָפְחָד

Vatikravnah b'not Tz'lofkhad

The daughters of Tz'lofkhad came forward (Numbers 27:1).

I DEDICATE THIS TEACHING to my parents, Dr. David Kligler and Dr. Deborah Kligler Krasnow, of blessed memory. My father was always completely supportive of my mother's academic and professional career. He encouraged her to finish her dissertation before they started a family. My mother's doctorate in sociology, completed in 1953, studied the effect of working women on the family. When my brothers and I were still quite young, my father again encouraged my mother to enter the workplace, and she began a long and satisfying career, serving for many years as the highly respected associate dean of Albert Einstein Medical School. My mother never trumpeted her accomplishments, but she raised three staunch feminists simply by the power of her example. Mom, this is for you!

We encounter a remarkable passage as *Sefer Bamidbar*, the book of Numbers, draws near its conclusion. The 40 years of wandering have passed, and the Children of Israel are approaching the banks of the Jordan

River. Miriam and Aaron have passed away, and Moses knows that his own death is approaching. A new generation has arisen during the decades of wandering, and they are preparing to claim their inheritance: the Promised Land. Soon, the manna will cease to fall and the cloud of glory will cease to guide them. The Children of Israel will need to claim the land and then work the land with their own efforts. They will need to follow the commandments without Moses to instruct them. Are they finally ready?

The daughters of Tz'lofkhad, descendants of Joseph, step forward. Their names are Makhlah, Noa, Hoglah, Milcah and Tirzah. They stand before Moses, and all the chieftains and leaders of Israel, and they say: "Our father died in the wilderness and left no sons. Shall he lose his inheritance of the land just because he has no male heirs? Give us a holding!"

The daughters' plea is unprecedented, and Moses does not know how to rule, so he inquires of God. "And YHVH said to Moses, 'The daughters of Tz'lofkhad speak rightly! . . . Transfer their father's share to them' " (Numbers 27:7).

I, along with countless other commentators, am struck by several elements of this passage. This is one of the rare passages in the Torah where women take center stage. And, these women take center stage with force. The language of the Torah emphasizes their assertiveness: וַתִּקְרַבְנָה *Vatikravnah*, they drew near; וַתַּעֲמֹדְנָה *Vata'amodnah*, they stood before the leadership at the Tent of Meeting; and they said תְּנָה־לָּנוּ אֲחֻזָּה *T'nah lanu akhuzah*, "Give us a holding!" (This is the command form of the verb; they are not asking, they are demanding!)

Equally unusual is God's response to the women's demand: כֵּן בְּנוֹת צְלָפְחָד דֹּבְרֹת! *Kein b'not Tz'lofkhad dovrot!*—"The daughters of Tz'lofkhad speak rightly!" Avivah Zornberg, in her book *Bewilderments: Reflections on the Book of Numbers*,[1] points out that this is the only time in the entire Torah when God enthusiastically affirms the words of any Israelite. The Children of Israel make many demands on their journey: תְּנוּ־לָנוּ מַיִם! *T'nu lanu mayim!*—"Give us water!" (Exodus 17:2); תְּנָה־לָּנוּ בָשָׂר! *T'nah lanu basar!*—"Give us meat!" (Numbers 11:13). These demands are accompanied by weeping and moaning, and always by a desire to go back to Egypt. God never affirms their demands, but rather criticizes and bemoans their constant complaints. The tone of Tz'lofkhad's daughters demand is clearly different: Give us the Promised Land! The daughters are not whining in

---

1. Avivah Zornberg, *Bewilderments: Reflections on the Book of Numbers*, 2015.

victimhood, they are claiming their power, and God can finally say כֵּן!—"Yes!"

Tz'lofkhad's daughters reappear in the final verses of the book of Numbers, on the banks of the Jordan, and are praised once again for their commitment and faith. On that note, the book of Numbers concludes. It is interesting to reflect that both at the beginning of the Exodus journey and now at the end, women take center stage. The exodus from Egypt is insured by the brave women of that episode: the midwives Shifrah and Puah, Moses's mother Yokheved and sister Miriam, Pharaoh's daughter and Moses's wife, Tziporah. And now, on the cusp of the Promised Land, Makhlah, Noa, Hoglah, Milkah and Tirtzah model the courage and faith that will be necessary to now cross the Jordan River.

Perhaps these women, whose appearance is so relatively rare in the Torah, appear at these key moments as the feminine archetypes and agents of choosing life, God's greatest desire for humanity. I also cheer for the daughters not as archetypes, but as determined women. We live in an age in which women are finding their voices and demanding their place at the table. May all women take inspiration from the daughters of Tz'lofkhad.

In addition, to me, the daughters of Tz'lofkhad represent the common person, the average citizen—the foot soldier, as it were. They have no special status. In fact, they are among the least enfranchised members of their society. Yet they approach the leaders directly, stand upright, and declare their complete readiness and right to participate in the challenges ahead. They are empowered.

This is what we need to enter a Promised Land, to make a better world. Every person, regardless of public station, must view himself or herself as a leader. Each one of us must ask ourselves: "What is needed here, and how am I equipped to make it happen?" Each one of us must locate and act upon our own reservoir of determination and courage. We can no longer wait to be told what to do, and then to complain about it.

Moses will soon be gone, and the Children of Israel must finally grow up and take full responsibility for their destiny as a people. The daughters of Tz'lofkhad lead the way. And God enthusiastically approves!

42

Matot | מטות

*Do Not Separate Yourself
From the Community*

וַיָּבֹאוּ בְנֵי־גָד וּבְנֵי רְאוּבֵן וַיֹּאמְרוּ אֶל־מֹשֶׁה . . . אִם־מָצָאנוּ
חֵן בְּעֵינֶיךָ יֻתַּן אֶת־הָאָרֶץ הַזֹּאת לַעֲבָדֶיךָ לַאֲחֻזָּה אַל־תַּעֲבִרֵנוּ
אֶת־הַיַּרְדֵּן:

*Va'yavo'u v'nei Gad uv'nei Reuven va'yomru el Moshe:
. . . "Im matzanu hein b'einekha, yutan et ha'aretz
ha'zot la'avadekha la'akhuzah; al ta'avireinu et
ha'Yardein."*

The men of Reuven and Gad came and said to Moses . . . "Do
us this favor and let us remain here; do not make us cross the
Jordan" (Numbers 32:2, 5).

AS WE APPROACH THE end of *Sefer Bamidbar*, the book of Numbers, the
children of Israel have conquered lands on the east side of the Jordan, the
plains of Moab, and are encamped there. They are anticipating completing
their long journey and crossing the Jordan River into the Promised Land.

At this point, the tribes of Reuven and Gad approach Moses and the leadership of the 12 tribes. They explain that Moab is cattle country, and that Reuven and Gad are cattle breeders. They want to settle here, rather than accompany the rest of the Israelites across the Jordan into Canaan.

Moses chastises them: "Are your brothers to go to war while you remain here? Do not take the heart out of your kinsmen as they prepare to cross over into the land that YHVH promised them!" (Numbers 32:6–7). Moses reminds them that a generation ago, their fathers had returned from scouting the Promised Land and discouraged the Children of Israel from entering the land. That incident resulted in 40 years of wandering. Moses insists that the tribes of Reuven and Gad must maintain solidarity with their kin: "If you turn away now . . . you will bring calamity upon the entire people!" (Numbers 32:15).

Reuven and Gad accept Moses's argument. They offer to send their troops across the Jordan with the rest of the Israelites and promise to return to these lands only after the land of Canaan across the Jordan has been secured. Moses accepts this compromise, and permits them to build towns for their families and pens for their flocks and herds. Only in solidarity will the Israelites be able to complete their journey. Gad and Reuven will not abandon them.

This story is, of course, emblematic of one of the unwavering principles of Judaism: the primacy of community. The "Wicked Child" in the Passover *Haggadah* is labeled as such because he does not think of himself as part of the community: "What does the wicked child say? 'What does all this ritual mean to you?' To you and not to him, for he has withdrawn himself from the community." The *Haggadah* explains that this behavior has dire consequences: "Had this child been in Egypt, he would not have been liberated [because he no longer identified with the Children of Israel]."

Had the tribes of Reuven and Gad decided long before this week's Torah portion that they liked the verdant pastures of the Land of Goshen back in Egypt, and did not want to leave slavery, then they, too, would not have been liberated. They would have opted out of the terror and exaltation of crossing the Red Sea, and of hearing the voice of God at Mount Sinai. They would not have had to declare, "We will do, and we will listen!" when asked to enter a moral covenant with YHVH, Life Unfolding. They would have avoided the trials of the sojourn in the wilderness, and the struggle and fulfillment of conquering the Promised Land.

Remaining committed to the Jewish People is a mixed bag, to say the least. One does not get to enjoy the blessings of being a Jew without also partaking in the difficulties. Of course, this is true of any committed relationship, and that is what Judaism asks of us: to be committed to one another and to our collective project of bringing holiness into the world. The Talmud declares, כָּל יִשְׂרָאֵל עֲרֵבִים זֶה בָּזֶה *Kol Yisrael areivim zeh bazeh*—"All Israel are responsible for one another" (Babylonian Talmud, Tractate Shevuot 39a) Hillel famously taught, אַל תִּפְרֹשׁ מִן הַצִּבּוּר *Al tifrosh min ha'tzibur*—"Do not separate yourself from the community" (Pirkei Avot 2:4).

In past eras, our solidarity was almost always enforced by external pressure. Because we were not accepted in the majority culture, we were forced to rely on each other. In modern times, those external restrictions have at times eased to the point where our affiliation to the Jewish whole has become almost entirely voluntary. Certainly, we American Jews are experiencing such a period. There is no Pharaoh to force us together against our will, and there is no Moses to bring us together through shared aspirations. The tribes of Reuven and Gad are free to go their own way without consequence. Like cowboys on the great frontier, shouldn't they be free to lead their herds wherever the grazing is good? Shouldn't we be free to follow our own goals and desires? Isn't that what freedom is all about?

This particularly American myth of the rugged individual, the self-made man (for this is a mostly masculine ideal) is a fallacy. YHVH frees the slaves not so that they might each go their own way seeking individual fulfillment, but so that they might together create a just society that is concerned with the well-being of all of its members. For Judaism, this is the purpose for which we were created. For Judaism, there is no "I" without a "We."

The Jewish emphasis on community is an antidote to our era's self-absorbed fantasies of unfettered individualism. I have met many non-Jews who are drawn to Judaism for precisely that reason; they yearn for a community where people are deeply invested in each other's lives. It is a classic irony: While many Jews are longing to escape what feels to them like an overbearing and suffocating community, others look in at us longingly, wishing to have what we often seek to escape.

In 1952, sociologists Mark Zborowski and Elizabeth Herzog wrote a classic study of Jewish shtetl life, *Life Is With People*. I have always loved that title. I think it captures the Jewish ethos perfectly.

My teacher, Rabbi Zalman Schachter-Shalomi, of blessed memory, liked to put it this way: "The only way to get it together is together." I'm sure Moses would agree; it's the only way we will get to the Promised Land.

43

Mas'ei | מסעי

The Inner Journey

אֵלֶּה מַסְעֵי בְנֵי־יִשְׂרָאֵל אֲשֶׁר יָצְאוּ מֵאֶרֶץ מִצְרָיִם

*Eileh mas'ei V'nei Yisrael asher yatz'u me'eretz
Mitzrayim*

These are the journeys of the Children of Israel after leaving
the Land of Egypt (Numbers 33:1).

AS WE REACH THE end of the book of *Bamidbar*, the Children of Israel
have arrived at the banks of the River Jordan. The Promised Land is just
on the other side. סֵפֶר דְּבָרִים *Sefer Devarim,* known in English as the book
of Deuteronomy, will complete the Five Books of Moses, but there is no
further journeying beyond the banks of the Jordan in that final book. The
epic journey that began with the book of Exodus has reached its destination. Fittingly, this final portion of *Bamidbar* is called *Mas'ei*—"Journeys,"
and it begins with a lengthy recounting of every encampment at which the
Children of Israel sojourned during the past 40 years.

How are we to read this chapter? As a list, it is pretty tedious. We
stopped here, and here, and here . . . but as I have endeavored to make clear
throughout these commentaries, the Torah is not a road atlas. It is rather a

map of our inner journey. It is the journey of the soul, as the *Haggadah* tells us, "from slavery to freedom, from anguish to joy, from darkness to light, from degradation to dignity."

Looking at the names of the Israelite encampments in that light, one becomes aware that the place names themselves are heavy with symbolism. Are they real places or states of being?

The very first destination sets the tone for this symbolic journey: "The Children of Israel set out from Ramses and encamped at Sukkot" (Numbers 33:5). רַעְמְסֵס *Ramses* is one of the fortified cities that Pharaoh forced the Children of Israel to construct. סֻכֹּת *Sukkot* means "temporary shelters." The first step of the journey is the willingness to leave the "fortified city" of the self behind, and instead to dwell in a *sukkah*, an open and fragile structure. This is the only way we can grow and change: by making ourselves vulnerable and open. Surely, there is comfort in staying behind the walls of a fortress, even if it also the place of imprisonment. But for those of us who sense that there is a calling greater than static safety, we must, despite our fears, risk opening ourselves to the unknown. We can only serve YHVH, Life Unfolding, if we give up our defenses. We cannot meet life on its own terms, find out who we really are, or discover the exhilarating essence of life if we never venture beyond our comfort zone. Perhaps this is "Rule No. 1" of the spiritual journey.

And it's not easy! Why do you think the Children of Israel constantly cry that they want to return to Egypt? Opening to life offers no guarantee of safety. We face an ongoing inner battle between choosing greater aliveness versus retreating into the constraints of fear. The famed Sufi poet Rumi wrote: "Moses and Pharaoh are both within you: You need to look for these two adversaries within yourself."

Many of the encampments that then follow in this chapter are named in evocative ways. For example, the Children of Israel journey on from Sukkot to פִּי הַחִירֹת *Pi HaKhirot*, which can mean "The Opening to Freedom." Elsewhere, they reach מָרָה *Marah*, "Bitterness," and later מִתְקָה *Mitkah*, "Sweetness." קִבְרֹת הַתַּאֲוָה *Kivrot Ha'Ta'avah* means "The Death of Craving;" חֲרָדָה *Haradah* is "Trembling;" and רְפִידִם *Rephidim* is interpreted as "Weakness." What stories might we weave about our sojourns in each of these places and the hard lessons learned at each stop along the way?

"These are the journeys of the Children of Israel . . . ." We are the Children of Israel, and so these are also our journeys, from constriction to expansiveness, and from fear to faith. Let's keep walking.

דברים
Deuteronomy

אינני עבר את־הירדן ואתם עברים וירשתם
את־הארץ הטובה הזאת

I will not cross the Jordan. You, however, will cross,
and you will inherit this good land. (Deuteronomy 4:22)

44 ———————————

Devarim | דברים

Finding Your Voice

בְּעֵבֶר הַיַּרְדֵּן בְּאֶרֶץ מוֹאָב הוֹאִיל מֹשֶׁה בֵּאֵר אֶת־הַתּוֹרָה
הַזֹּאת

*B'eiver ha'Yardein b'eretz Moav ho'il Moshe bei'eir et
hatorah hazot*

On the far side of the Jordan, in the land of Moab, Moses
undertook to explain this Torah (Deuteronomy 1:5).

THE ENGLISH NAME OF the fifth and final book of the Five Books of
Moses is Deuteronomy. "Deuteronomy" is a Greek term that means "repetition of the law." This is an appropriate name, as the entire book—save the
very end that describes Moses's passing—is a recounting by Moses of the
three previous books of the Torah. The book is in the form of a very long
final oration by Moses, in which he recaps the journey of the Children of
Israel under his leadership and repeats and expands upon the *mitzvot*—the
laws by which the Jewish People will live.

The Hebrew name of the book, דְּבָרִים *Devarim*, is also an appropriate
title, and a more evocative one as well. *Devarim* means "words." The book
of *Devarim* is filled with Moses's words. This is the same Moses who, when

called decades earlier by YHVH at the burning bush, could only respond, בִּ֣ אֲדֹנָ֣י לֹ֣א אִ֣ישׁ דְּבָרִים֙ אָנֹ֔כִי *Bi, Adonai, lo ish devarim anokhi . . .* —"Please, my Lord, I am not a man of words—not now, not ever—I am heavy of speech and heavy of tongue" (Exodus 4:10).

I am not the first to notice that Moses, who originally insists that he is not a man of words, is able at the end of his life to deliver a 33-chapter summation and explication of his life's mission. What a transformation! How did Moses "find his voice?"

The Sefat Emet, Rabbi Yehudah Leib Alter of Ger (1847–1905), points us to the double meaning of the word *be'eir* in the verse I cited above: *Ho'il Moshe bei'eir et hatorah hazot.* The plain meaning of this verse is, "Moses undertook to explain this Torah." The verb בֵּאֵר *bei'eir* means "explain, expound, elucidate." But the noun בְּאֵר *bei'eir* means "a well." Thus, a creative alternate meaning dances in the background: "Moses undertook to well up this Torah."

Listen: "On the far side of the Jordan, in the land of Moab, this Torah welled up in Moses."

Where does inspiration dwell? Is it on some distant mountaintop, or is it deep within each of us? Perhaps Moses, earlier in life, did not yet know how to let words well up within his soul. The Sefat Emet continues the analogy and compares those who mistakenly think of themselves as a "sealed cistern" or a "holding tank" (בּוֹר *bor* in Hebrew) to those who correctly understand themselves to be a "well" (בְּאֵר *bei'eir*). A cistern or a tank is a closed system; once its contents have been emptied, it is dry. It does not refill from within or below, but only at the whims of the unpredictable rain. A well is an open system; it taps into a rechargeable, invisible, ever-flowing source. A good well brims over and never runs dry. Therefore, if a person thinks of herself as a cistern, she mistakenly thinks that inspiration is a product of her own self and a limited resource. The wellsprings of creativity will not replenish this person. But one who sees oneself as a well comes to understand that he is not the source, but rather a conduit for inspiration.

Playing further with the Hebrew, one can say that the difference between a בּוֹר *bor* and a בְּאֵר *bei'eir* is the vivifying א *aleph*, the Voice of God, the soundless letter from which the remainder of the alphabet, and thus human communication, emerges. Without our connection to the deep, flowing silence of the *aleph*, our inspiration will run dry.

Prior to encountering the presence of YHVH, Life Unfolding, at the burning bush, Moses labored under the illusion that hampers so many of us in our search for a life of purpose. He thought that he was a closed system, limited to his own resources and resourcefulness. At the burning bush, Moses's illusory aloneness was shattered, and he became a messenger, a channel, a vessel for a greater calling. He would find his voice by, paradoxically, allowing inspiration to flow through him. We find this understanding in YHVH's response to Moses at the burning bush. When Moses stammers, "I am slow of speech and slow of tongue!" YHVH replies: "Who gives humans speech? . . . Now go, and I will be with you, in your mouth, and will teach you what to say" (Exodus 4:11).

Over the next 40 years, Moses learns how to allow God to speak through him. Is this what it means to be a prophet? Perhaps. I think it is what it means to be an artist. And a lover. When we learn how to dig down in ourselves beyond our egos to the wellsprings of inspiration that flow for all of us, when we tend our well so that we can water others from our particular channel to the Divine, we are liberated from the illusion of our separateness while simultaneously fulfilling our own unique role in the universe.

By the time Moses speaks *Sefer Devarim,* the "Book of Words," he has mastered the subtle skill of allowing words to well up in him. He becomes the well. The teachings flow from his lips. Indeed, as his oration reaches its climax at the end of Deuteronomy, Moses does his utmost to imbue the Children of Israel with the understanding that they, too, are wells and not cisterns, and will be able to continue to connect with the Divine after Moses is gone:

> [This teaching] is not in the heavens, that you should say, "Who among us can go up to the heavens and get it for us and impart it to us, that we may do it?" Nor is it beyond the sea, that you should say, "Who among us can cross to the other side of the sea and get it for us, and impart it to us, that we may do it?" No, the word is in your mouth and in your heart, that you may do it (Deuteronomy 30:11–14).

Across a lifetime of struggle and service, Moses came to trust and to allow inspiration to flow through him. He found his voice, and his words resound in the world to this day. He also left us with a charge, as all great teachers will do: Do not think that creative and moral inspiration is some limited resource, secreted in some external, inaccessible source. No, that source flows all around you and within you, waiting to be tapped, ready to well up in your being and flow out into the world.

45

Va'et'khanan | ואתחנן

The Choosing People

כִּי עַם קָדוֹשׁ אַתָּה לַיהוָה אֱלֹהֶיךָ בְּךָ בָּחַר יְהוָה אֱלֹהֶיךָ לִהְיוֹת
לוֹ לְעַם סְגֻלָּה מִכֹּל הָעַמִּים אֲשֶׁר עַל־פְּנֵי הָאֲדָמָה:

*Ki am kadosh atah l'YHVH Elohekha; b'kha bakhar
YHVH Elohekha lih'yot lo l'am s'gulah mikol ha'amim
asher al p'nei ha'adamah.*

For you are a people consecrated to YHVH your God; YHVH
your God chose you as a treasured people from among all the
peoples of the earth (Deuteronomy 7:6).

THE PORTION OF *VA'ET'KHANAN* contains some of the best-known
and important passages in the Torah. Moses recounts for the Children of
Israel the events of almost 40 years earlier, when they stood at Mount Sinai,
and repeats The Ten Commandments for them. Next, Moses proclaims,
שְׁמַע יִשְׂרָאֵל יְהוָה אֱלֹהֵינוּ יְהוָה אֶחָד: *Sh'ma Yisrael, Adonai Eloheinu, Adonai
Ekhad!*—"Hear, O Israel, YHVH is our God, YHVH is One!" and tells the
Children of Israel to love YHVH with all of their heart, soul and might.

In addition, Moses reminds the Children of Israel of another central assertion of the Torah: God has chosen them from among all the nations to be God's especially treasured people.

For many modern Jews, the idea of our "chosen-ness" is problematic at best and abhorrent at worst. This is a specifically modern dilemma; only in very recent times have we begun to conceptualize ourselves as belonging to a global human family. But prior to this modern idea taking hold, all peoples understood themselves to be in a special and central relationship with the cosmos, and with their deity or deities. Just to give one example, the Navajo call themselves the Diné, meaning simply "The People" or "Children of the Holy People." This self-understanding did not necessarily lead to the conclusion that other peoples were "sub-human," but it did mean that only the People themselves were the central actors in maintaining the cosmic order. The ancient Jews were no different in this regard. In the Middle Ages, however, Christians claimed that the Jewish People's chosen status had been superseded by their own selection by God, and the Jews' claim of chosen-ness was used as a cudgel against them. Jews responded by defending their chosen status as a badge of pride and a source of comfort in their debased circumstances.

But for progressive Jewish thinkers of the 20th century, the concept that a Creator God would choose one people to treasure out of all the cultures and peoples of the world became unpalatable and out of step with the emerging idea of us being one human family. The emerging scientific worldview that defines the modern era called into question the very idea of a willful supernatural deity who directed human affairs and could choose one people over another. If Jews desired to fit in to this modern world, despite all the forces arrayed against us, a claim to be specially chosen looked like a claim of superiority to others. It was an uncomfortable and dissonant legacy to carry into the modern world. Many Jews distanced themselves from this claim and apologized for it.

What to do? Some proposed that "chosen-ness" could be reinterpreted to fit modern sensibilities. There is support for varying interpretations in the Torah itself. In the book of Exodus, as the Children of Israel gather at the base of Mount Sinai, God makes clear that their special status is contingent on their behavior:

> If you obey Me faithfully and keep my covenant, then you shall
> be my treasured possession among all the peoples (Exodus 19:5).

In this passage, the Torah makes clear that there is nothing inherently superior about us as a people. We have, rather, been chosen to fulfill a covenant—a sacred relationship with the Creator. We have been chosen to fulfill a mission, and a very exalted and demanding one at that. As Isaiah famously expresses it:

> I, YHVH, have called you in righteousness and taken you by the hand. I created you and gave you my covenant: to be a light to the nations, to open eyes that are blind, to bring the prisoner out of confinement, to bring out of the dungeon those who sit in darkness (Isaiah 42:6–7).

This concept of having a special mission could be adapted into a modern context. Firstly, it is conditional on our behavior: We must act as a light to the nations, or we have failed at the task for which God chose us. Secondly, it does not claim superiority: There is nothing inherently superior about the Jews, but we have been chosen for a unique mission. Thirdly, it is a universal mission: to serve all of humanity by demonstrating through our behavior the truth of the moral law that underpins the cosmos. The Reform movement embraced this idea and called it "ethical monotheism."

But for other modern religious thinkers, most famously Rabbi Mordecai M. Kaplan, the very idea of chosen-ness was obsolete. Kaplan, in framing his approach to Judaism that he termed "Reconstructionism," rejected the concept of a supernatural deity. For Kaplan, God was an impersonal force, an infinite creative process that imbued us humans with a sense of purpose and reverence for life. For Kaplan, the idea of a deity who singles out and chooses certain human beings over others was patently absurd. Kaplan held that Judaism—and all cultures and religions—are human products, the striving of human beings to discern and articulate their sense of purpose and place in the universe. Thus, even the Torah is a record of our searching for God, not a Divine document but an inspired human effort. Kaplan insisted that it was our duty to "reconstruct" our traditions and concepts to make them meaningful and relevant to our evolving understanding of the universe.

Kaplan, therefore, rejected outright the notion that we needed to perpetuate our claim to be the Chosen People. For both practical and theological reasons, Kaplan held that chosen-ness had no place in the modern world. We could still retain our sense of having a special calling without having to claim a unique or superior status relative to other peoples and cultures. Kaplan's radical position on this question caused an uproar in the

Jewish world—so much of our identity as Jews was (and perhaps still is) wrapped up in thinking of ourselves as "special"—yet his logic, if you accept the premises of modern scientific thought, is hard to refute.

In Mordecai Kaplan's America of the mid-20th century, there was still much to bind the Jewish community together, even in the absence of a supernatural Divine calling. We were a largely immigrant community, most of us still connected by customs and language and memories of the old country. Anti-Semitism was an external force that pushed us together, and kept us reliant on one another and on the Jewish community at large. The project of Zionism galvanized us, giving a new, nationalist sense of mission to our collective efforts. Maybe we no longer needed to be "The Chosen People" as the organizing principle of our shared peoplehood. There was so much else that bound us together.

Now, however, in the 21st century, much of this connective tissue of Jewish life has weakened dramatically: the immigrant ties that bound our parents and grandparents have dissipated; the oppressive force of anti-Semitism is muted enough here in the United States that it does not force us into a sense of shared necessity to stick together; even Zionism no longer inspires our fervent solidarity and sense of common cause.

Thus, progressive Jewish communities are left scrambling for a principle that would bind us together. For so many of us, considering ourselves "chosen" no longer compels allegiance and participation in Jewish life. What then might today serve as a principle or center of gravity that might continue to draw us to Jewish community?

I propose that our center of gravity can be Judaism itself. Judaism provides an ancient and grounding path in a fragmented and ungrounded world. Judaism is a moral beacon cutting through the fog of modern life. Judaism trains us to perceive the sacredness of existence beneath the profane commodification of the earth. Judaism honors ancestors and links us to future generations. Judaism brings us together with other seekers of the good and the true.

For those of us who no longer believe in a supernatural God who chose us, I propose that it is now time for us to be not the Chosen People, but the Choosing People. We choose to walk the path of Judaism. Not because Judaism is more special than other cultural and spiritual paths, but because the particular gifts of the Jewish path enrich us and enrich the world. We choose Judaism to honor those who went through fire and water to keep our heritage alive. We choose Judaism out of love and not compulsion. We choose Judaism because it continuously reminds us to identify with the stranger and the powerless, and to practice compassion and kindness. We choose Judaism because it is a path of heart, acknowledging life's complexity while still choosing and celebrating life.

We choose Judaism because Judaism elevates the concepts of Justice and Mercy to positions of cosmic importance. We choose Judaism because it teaches that every individual matters. And much, much more—I trust that many readers are thinking of their own reasons that bring them to cherish Judaism and cherish being a Jew. And we choose to share the Jewish path with all who are drawn to it. We welcome them, even if they are not of Jewish heritage. We hold that anyone who chooses to walk this Jewish path with us has every right to become one of the "Choosing People."

As Moses will tell us later in Deuteronomy, this choice is not in heaven nor across the sea, but in our own mouths and hearts. The choice is ours.

46 —————————————————

Eikev | עקב

Gratitude

וְאָכַלְתָּ וְשָׂבָעְתָּ וּבֵרַכְתָּ

V'akhalta v'savata u'veirakhta

You shall eat, and be satiated, and give thanks (Deuteronomy 8:10).

AS SOME OF YOU may know, those three Hebrew words—*V'akhalta v'savata u'veirakhta*—comprise the proof text for the בִּרְכַּת הַמָזוֹן *Birkat Ha'mazon*, known in English as the "Grace After Meals." *Birkat Ha'mazon* is a very long series of blessings of gratitude that are meant to be recited—and are often sung boisterously—after every meal. In addition to offering blessings before eating, such as the *Motzi*, the blessing over bread, our sages determined from this verse of Torah that we should also give thanks after we eat. Their decision was based on the order of the words: eat, be satiated, then give thanks!

Why should we be required to give thanks after we eat? The verses in Deuteronomy that immediately follow explain that when you have entered the good land that YHVH is giving to you and have plenty to eat, and have built fine houses to live in, and you have become prosperous, "beware lest

179

your heart grow haughty ... and you say to yourselves, 'it was my own power and strength that won this wealth for me!' " No, you must remember that your abundance is a gift from God, the Source of All (from Deuteronomy 8:11–17).

The Torah, as always, understands human nature. When we are famished or thirsty, and someone offers us refreshment, we might find ourselves exclaiming, unbidden, "Oh, thank God!" with a sigh, knowing that imminent relief to our suffering has arrived. But when we are satiated, we quickly forget the need we so desperately carried just moments earlier. That's the way we are. We get used to our good fortune and our privilege, assume that as our baseline, and then focus on our next need. We forget to give thanks.

I recently read about a study that explored how quickly people become accustomed to new circumstances. For example, when we get faster internet speed, how long does it take before we expect that speed all the time? How long before we find ourselves complaining when the speed is too slow, when just a short time ago we were thrilled with our computer's new capacity? It takes almost no time at all. And from there, it is but a small and predictable step to feeling unsatisfied, having forgotten completely about our blessed good fortune.

Therefore, Judaism instructs us to practice gratitude before the need is met and after the need is met—in other words, all the time! Gratitude is the antidote to dissatisfaction. It is impossible to *kvetch* and keep a straight face when you dwell in a moment of appreciation.

You shall eat, and be satiated, and give thanks. When a physical need is involved, the feeling of satiation comes only after the need is met. But with spiritual and emotional needs, the reverse is true. If you can fill yourself with gratitude, lacks that you may have felt a moment before disappear! It is quite wonderful: When I am counting my blessings—when I am focusing on all the good that is bestowed upon me in any moment—at that moment, I lack nothing. I fill and overflow with gratefulness. My cup runneth over.

Prayer is designed to carry us into this blessed state. You can do it right now; you can still your unquiet spirit, you can silence your endless whining simply by noticing the unearned bounty that has been bestowed upon you in this moment. Notice the next breath that has been granted to you, gaze at the greenery outside your window, feel the pulse sending life through your veins and arteries. These are gifts to you from the Universe. Give thanks! These infinite gifts cannot be bought or sold; they are literally priceless. They have been freely given. And the only way we can even begin to return this kindness is with gratitude, freely offered.

47 ──────────────────────────────

Re'eih | ראה

Open Your Hand

פָּתֹחַ תִּפְתַּח אֶת־יָדְךָ לְאָחִיךָ לַעֲנִיֶּךָ וּלְאֶבְיֹנְךָ בְּאַרְצֶךָ׃

*Pato'akh tiftakh et yadkha l'akhikha, l'aniyekha
u'le'evyonkha b'artzekha.*

You must open, open your hand to the poor and to the needy
in your land (Deuteronomy 15:11).

SOMETIMES, THE TORAH REVEALS its deeper meanings to us through
elaborate interpretation and subtle analysis. At other times, Torah speaks to
us directly across the millennia, with little need for mediation. Our passage
this week falls in this latter category; here is my lightly adapted translation:

> If there is a needy person among you . . . do not harden your heart
> and shut your hand against your needy fellow. Rather, open, yes,
> open your hand, and lend, yes, lend sufficiently to meet their need.
> Watch yourself, lest you harbor the base thought, "I will never
> see this loan repaid." Give, give readily, and have no regrets when
> you do so. And as a result, YHVH will bless you in all of your ef-
> forts and all of your undertakings. For there will always be needy
> among you, and therefore I command you: open, open your hand
> to the poor and to the needy in your land (Deuteronomy 15:7–11).

Biblical Hebrew, when it needs to be emphatic, repeats verbs twice. In this passage, we see: "open, open your hand"; "lend, lend sufficiently to meet their need"; "give, give readily"; and then, in typical biblical poetic structure, "open, open your hand" repeated again to complete the passage. I love the incantatory flow of it: "open, open, lend, lend, give, give, open, open."

I also appreciate the way that the Torah invokes Pharaoh when it says, "Do not harden your heart and shut your hand against your needy fellow." Pharaoh of the hardened heart and the closed fist is the archetype of resistance to Life Unfolding. Pharaoh is the embodiment of everything we are trying not to become as we aim towards the Promised Land. In next week's portion, *Shoftim*, Moses instructs the people that one day, when they have finally settled in the Promised Land, they will want to set a king over themselves. Moses warns them that this king must guard himself carefully, so he does not become like Pharaoh. This future king "must not send his people back to Egypt just so that he can accumulate more horses"—that is, he cannot enslave his people for the sake of increasing his wealth—"for YHVH has warned you: 'Do not go back that way again!' " (Deuteronomy 17:16). On the map of our spiritual growth, the Land of Pharaoh is the land of hardened hearts and closed fists. We must not regress; we must not go back that way again.

The path towards a compassionate self and society requires material and spiritual generosity. The Torah promises a reward for this behavior: "YHVH will bless you in all of your efforts and all of your undertakings." I understand this not as a literal tit-for-tat, but rather as the beautiful consequence of living with a malleable heart and with open hands: I then can become a vessel through which the energy of Life Unfolding can freely flow. As that energy flows through me, I am indeed truly blessed.

Parashat Re'eih always falls close to *Rosh Hodesh Elul*, the new moon of Elul. This new moon heralds the approach of Rosh Hashanah, one moon from now, and so initiates the season of תְּשׁוּבָה *teshuvah*, of our return and recommitment to the path of truth, integrity and love. *Re'eih* is timed perfectly to remind us that the first step towards our goal is to unclench our fists and give of ourselves freely. Open, yes, open your hand.

48

Shoftim | שפטים

Justice, Justice

צֶדֶק צֶדֶק תִּרְדֹּף

Tzedek, tzedek tirdof

Justice, justice you shall pursue (Deuteronomy 16:20).

THIS IS ONE OF the central declarations and core *mitzvot* of the Torah. The entire passage reads:

> You shall appoint magistrates and officials for your tribes, in all the settlements that YHVH your God is giving you, and they shall govern the people with due justice. You shall not be partial in judgment; hear out low and high alike. Decide justly between the Israelite and the stranger alike. Take no bribe, for bribes blind the eyes of the discerning and upset the plea of the just. Justice, justice you shall pursue . . . (Deuteronomy 16:18–20).

This is a central theme of our Torah and is repeated in various sets of instructions throughout the five books. For example, in Exodus, we read YHVH's charge to the people:

> You shall not subvert the rights of your needy in their disputes. Keep far from a false charge; do not bring death on those who are

innocent and in the right for I will not acquit the wrongdoer. Do not take bribes, for bribes blind the clear-sighted and upset the pleas of those who are in the right. Do not oppress the stranger, for you know the soul of the stranger, having yourselves been strangers in the land of Egypt (Exodus 23:6–8).

The pursuit of justice has, from the beginning, been a fundamental tenet of Judaism. Perhaps our origin as slaves sensitized us to this principle. Over the millennia, a deeply thoughtful, detailed and sensitive discussion emerged as generations of Jewish thinkers expanded and expounded upon the question of what it means to treat everyone justly and fairly.

Tzedek, tzedek tirdof. In true Jewish fashion, let's take this phrase apart one word at a time and see what insights emerge. We begin with the word *tzedek.* Hebrew is a language based on root words; out of the root, many words are created, all of which share a cluster of related meanings. צֶדֶק *Tzedek* means "justice" or "righteousness"—that is, doing the right thing. One of its close relatives is צְדָקָה *tzedakah*, usually translated in English as "charity." Linguistically and conceptually, however, there is a critical distinction between the terms. "Charity" is derived from the Latin *caritas*, which means "love" or "regard." Charity is an act of love, of giving freely. *Tzedakah*, on the other hand, is an act of justice, understood by Jews to be a duty. The intention of giving *tzedakah* is to help manifest a basic Jewish goal: to enable every person to live with dignity because every person has been created in the image of God. If you can give out of love, so much the better, says Jewish law; but you give first of all because it is the right thing to do.

There is another word from the same root that you may recognize—צַדִּיק *tzaddik*. A *tzaddik*, a righteous person, is one who has embodied the quality of *tzedek*, treats people equitably and pursues justice as a matter of course. A *tzaddik* understands that all people are reflections of the Divine and has placed himself or herself entirely in service of bringing *tzedek* into the world.

The second word, תִּרְדֹּף *tirdof*, means "pursue." Why are we told to pursue justice, rather than simply to achieve justice? Commandments in the Torah do not equivocate; they simply tell us what we must do. In fact, we are instructed to pursue only two commandments in the entire body of *mitzvot*: צֶדֶק צֶדֶק תִּרְדֹּף *Tzedek, tzedek tirdof*—"Justice, justice you shall pursue"—and בַּקֵּשׁ שָׁלוֹם וְרָדְפֵהוּ *Bakeish shalom v'rodfeihu*—"Seek peace and pursue it" (Psalm 34:15). How interesting that justice and peace are considered pursuits, rather than concrete achievements! In the Jewish view, peace and justice exist as ideals for which we strive, but neither is attainable in ideal or permanent form here in our morally complex and ever-changing world. To attain perfect justice would mean that we not only have the ability to see every side of a conflict, but even the ability to predict the unfolding ramifications of each decision we render. This infinite perspective is simply beyond our ken as limited beings. This is the provenance of God, one of whose names in Jewish tradition is דַּיָּן אֱמֶת *Dayan Emet*—the True Judge. We know the terror and tyranny that result whenever humans ascribe to themselves the power to proclaim absolute justice or keep an absolute peace. We know that even our best judgments are inevitably fraught with unknowns and with unintended consequences.

And so, our tradition instructs us to humbly pursue, rather than to triumphantly attain, justice. Our sincere and wholehearted pursuit of this elusive goal elevates us and dignifies all those around us. There is no final arrival (at least not until the Messiah comes, so say some); it is the pursuit in which we are commanded to engage.

Finally, why is *tzedek* repeated in the phrase, *Tzedek, tzedek tirdof*? Would it not have been sufficient for the Torah to declare, *Tzedek tirdof*—"Justice you shall pursue?" Reish Lakish, who lived and taught in Tiberias in the third century C.E., taught that the repetition of *tzedek* in the phrase we are analyzing is to remind us to be deliberate and careful in judgment, revisiting and reviewing the case, and not rushing into a decision. (In Jewish law, a *beit din*, or rabbinical court, waits until the next day before delivering a guilty verdict.) Similarly, Maimonides, living in Egypt in the 12th century C.E., taught that the repetition emphasizes the need to consult with others, garnering as many points of view as possible before reaching a decision.

Others have argued that the term is repeated to convey the idea that the pursuit of justice is not only the responsibility of the officials and the courts, but also of each individual. As was taught in the name of Rabbi Hiyya, a fourth-century scholar, "If a person is neither a scholar, nor a teacher, nor known for observing all the ritual commandments, but stands up to protest against evil, such a person is considered a blessing."

Still others in the Talmud explain the repetition of "justice" refers to the need for just compromise. It is understood that often, two justified claims clash with each other; thus, *tzedek, tzedek*. The rabbis explained that the repetition of *tzedek* teaches us that when two justified claims clash with each other, the just solution is for the parties to find a compromise between them.

Bakhya ben Asher, living in Spain in the 12th century, taught that the double emphasis means justice under any circumstance, whether to your profit or loss, whether in word or in action, whether to Jew or non-Jew.

In 19th-century Poland, Reb Yaakov Yitkhak of P'shischa interpreted the word's repetition to connote that the end does not justify the means: "The pursuit of justice must also be done justly, unblemished by invalid means, with lies and surreptitiousness as some permit themselves under the flag of the worthy cause."

All this, from one extra word! And here, in North America in the 21st century, the words still compel us. How do we pursue justice in our lives and in our society today? I must admit to a sense of despair and fatigue as I witness the political climate of our country. (I resonate these days with Lily Tomlin's line, "No matter how cynical you become, it's never enough to keep up.") What is happening to our society's ideals of mutual responsibility? What can I do?

The wording of the *mitzvah* is very important now: We are commanded to pursue justice, even if the attainment of justice seems remote. Don't give up; your actions make a difference. It is incumbent upon us to reach beyond our sense of gloom or apathy, and to continue our sacred pursuit of creating a just and righteous civilization. Remember the words of Rabbi Tarfon: "It is not up to you to complete the task, but neither are you free to desist from it." (Pirkei Avot, 2:21).

In fact, every single day is filled with opportunities to treat people ethically and fairly, to give the benefit of the doubt, to stand up against injustice, to enact just solutions, to do the right thing. In every human exchange, with loved ones and with strangers, with clients and with customers, with employees and with bosses, we can make it our goal to bring more *tzedek* into the world. May each of us give *tzedakah*, pursue *tzedek* and strive to become a *tzaddik*. In private or in public, in large or small ways, may each of us keep choosing to do the right thing.

49 ———————————————————

Ki Teitzei | כי תצא

A Living Tradition

לֹא־תִרְאֶה אֶת־חֲמוֹר אָחִיךָ אוֹ שׁוֹרוֹ נֹפְלִים בַּדֶּרֶךְ וְהִתְעַלַּמְתָּ
מֵהֶם הָקֵם תָּקִים עִמּוֹ:

*Lo tir'eh et hamor akhikha o shoro noflim ba'derekh
v'hitalamta mei'hem; hakeim takim imo.*

If you see your fellow's ox or ass fallen on the road, do not
ignore it; you must raise it together (Deuteronomy 22:4).

KI TEITZEI CONTAINS MORE *mitzvot*—more commandments—than
any other portion in the Torah. In fact, there are no stories in *Ki Teitzei*,
only laws. Maimonides counts 72 discrete commandments that originate
in this *parashah*.

The laws in *Ki Teitzei* describe the needs and conditions of an ancient agrarian society, radically different from our own. We read about the
proper treatment of women captured as spoils of war; harsh punishment
for rebellious sons; what to do with a lost ox or sheep. The novice student
of Torah will wonder what relevance these instructions could possibly have
to contemporary life. Many a bar mitzvah boy and bat mitzvah girl have

188

despaired upon reading this as their assigned portion, knowing that they were somehow supposed to find a message in it.

But the novice does not yet understand that in Judaism, Torah is not a static document locked in time, but rather, a living tradition. The laws of the Torah are the basis of a 3,000-years-and-counting exploration of the deepest meaning and best application of the commandments. "Jewish Law" is not contained in the Torah; "Jewish Law" is the ever-evolving debate and interpretation of the Torah by Jewish scholars. Some of the commandments in *Ki Teitzei* become the foundation for entire areas of Jewish law and ethics, and occupy entire tractates of the Talmud. Some that are found too harsh or offensive are marginalized and shunted aside by Jewish tradition. Others remain the object of fierce debate to this day.

When read and studied in this light, the significance of portions like *Ki Teitzei* as the basis of Jewish law becomes apparent. Some examples:

> If you see your fellow's ox or ass fallen on the road, do not ignore it; you must raise it together (Deuteronomy 22:4).

> If you chance upon a bird's nest . . . do not take the mother together with her young. Send the mother off before you take the young for food . . . (Deuteronomy 22:7).

> You shall not muzzle an ox while it is threshing (Deuteronomy 25:4).

These laws, scattered through the text, become the proof texts in the Talmud for an entire category of Jewish law that the rabbis name צַעַר בַּעֲלֵי חַיִּים *Tza'ar Ba'alei Hayim*, "the suffering of living things," better translated as "the ethical treatment of animals." The rabbis endeavor to create a "balance between simultaneously permitting the use of animals for human need and prohibiting unnecessary cruelty to animals."[1] The ethical imperative to minimize suffering to animals extends to the laws of kosher slaughter; to rules that limit the overworking of animals (the fourth of the Ten Commandments insists that domesticated animals, as well as humans, must receive a Sabbath); and to showing compassion for all creatures, such as the mother bird cited above.

In contemporary Jewish thought, the evolution of Jewish law regarding ethical treatment of animals continues: Is factory farming kosher? Is

---

1. See this article for a great summary of *Tza'ar Ba'alei Hayim*: myjewishlearning.com/article/ethical-treatment-of-animals-in-judaism.

vegetarianism or even veganism the logical next step in our acknowledgment that animals are sentient and have feelings?

> You shall not abuse a needy and destitute laborer ... You must pay the wages due [the laborer] on the same day, before the sun sets (Deuteronomy 24:14–15).
>
> You must have completely honest weights, and completely honest measures (Deuteronomy 25:15).

These commandments form the foundation of Jewish business ethics, an enormous focus of Jewish law. The Jewish legal tradition pays at least as much attention to the *kashrut* (acceptability) of what we may or may not do in economic practices as it does to the *kashrut* of what we may or may not eat. As one teacher of mine put it, as Jews we should be more concerned about what comes out of our mouths than we are about what goes into our mouths! For those of us concerned with ethical labor and business laws, we can trace a direct line back to the Torah.

> If you see your fellow's ox or sheep gone astray, do not ignore it; you must take it back to them ... If you do not know who the owner is, you shall bring it home until the owner claims it; then you shall give it back ... you shall do the same with anything that someone loses and that you find: you must not remain indifferent (Deuteronomy 22:1–3).

Respecting others' property is critical to maintaining the trust that allows a society to thrive. Here again, the Talmud takes these general principles in the Torah and explores every possible nuance of what is considered "lost property," and what our responsibilities are to those who have lost it. When can we claim something that we found as our own? When is keeping something we've found theft? To what lengths should we go to locate the owner? The plethora of detailed debate in the Talmud can make your head spin, but without clear property laws, only the law of the jungle will prevail. In our digital age, these questions remain urgent: If we glean someone else's intellectual property or creative work from the internet, what do we owe them? We will find that Judaism has much to teach us in this regard.

ఇసి

> When you build a new house, you shall construct a railing around
> your roof, for if someone fell from your roof you would bear guilt
> (Deuteronomy 22:8).

To this day around the Mediterranean, many homes have flat roofs. In biblical times, the rooftop was part of the living space, and much activity took place on the roof. Thus, a railing was a practical safety measure. This specific law from our portion becomes the foundation for another basic Jewish ethical principle: We are each responsible for public safety. For I can easily imagine the homeowner's complaint: "How can the law require me to put up a railing? It's my home!" Judaism is non-negotiable: We must consider the well-being of others.

Again, Jewish tradition offers valuable guidance for contemporary issues. I was approached by a Jewish family that did not want to vaccinate their children because they believed that the vaccinations were harmful. In order to satisfy their children's school, they needed to prove that their religious beliefs would prevent them from vaccinating. I could not write such a letter. After studying the issue, I concluded that even if there was a marginal risk that the vaccines might injure the children, the Jewish imperative to protect public health vastly outweighed the potential risk to the individual. The commandment to put a railing around one's roof becomes both the formative precedent and the metaphor for our responsibility to the greater community. We are all in this together.

A well-known rabbinic parable humorously captures Judaism's emphasis on public safety: Some people were sitting in a boat, when one of them took a drill and began to bore under his seat. The other passengers protested to him, "What are you doing?" He said to them, "What has this to do with you? Am I not boring the hole under my own seat?" They retorted, "But the water will come in and drown us all!" (*Vayikra Rabbah* 4:6, fifth century C.E.).

ఇసి

Finally, here is an example of the Jewish legal tradition marginalizing a law that was deemed too harsh:

> If a parent has a rebellious and defiant son, who does not heed his
> father or mother and does not obey them even after they discipline

him, his father and mother shall take hold of him and bring him to the public square . . . They shall say to the town elders, this son of ours is disloyal and defiant, he does not heed us, he is a glutton and a drunkard. Thereupon the townspeople shall stone him to death (Deuteronomy 21:18–21).

Now, I know many of us parents have had the urge to drag our rebellious adolescent into the town square and do something similar, but even though the Torah regularly invokes capital punishment for crimes, later Jewish legal authorities held a profoundly negative opinion of the death penalty. So, even though the law was already "on the books," so to speak, Rabbinic Judaism interpreted every word of the law so restrictively as to make it impossible to prosecute. They declared that this law could only apply when the son was between the age of 13 and 13¼, that the mother and father's testimony must exactly corroborate, that the son must be proven a repeated glutton and drunkard, and much more, reducing the commandment to an absurdity.[2] Further, the rabbis (with no actual proof) stated that even in the time of the Torah the law had never been invoked, as a way of further delegitimizing the text without contradicting it outright.

Thus, we see that Torah—rather than being the immutable "truth" as some depict it—has always, in fact, been a malleable living document. While the Torah's elevated principles grew into the fabric of Jewish law and life, aspects of Torah that future generations found unpalatable were actively sidelined. Judaism is still evolving today, but the ongoing humane and progressive interpretation of Torah is never a given. It is truly up to each generation to study the chain of tradition and carry the values of Judaism into the future. *Ki Teitzei* offers a rich resource from which to begin.

---

2. See this article for a great summary of the treatment of the rebellious son: *jewish-virtuallibrary.org/rebellious-son.*

50

Ki Tavo | כי תבוא

The Inner Witness

אָרוּר מַכֵּה רֵעֵהוּ בַּסָּתֶר וְאָמַר כָּל־הָעָם אָמֵן:

*Arur makeih rei'eihu ba'sater—v'amar kol ha'am
"Amen."*

Cursed be the one who strikes down their fellow in secret—
and all the people shall say, "Amen" (Deuteronomy 27:24).

In *Ki Tavo*, Moses tells the Children of Israel the details of some of the rituals that they must perform once they cross the River Jordan and enter the Promised Land. Chapter 27 describes a unique communal reaffirmation of the covenant. The 12 tribes are to gather in the northern city of Shechem, where Jacob had settled long ago. Shechem sits in a valley between two hills, Mount Ebal and Mount Gerizim. Six tribes are to gather on the slopes of Ebal, and six on the slopes of Gerizim. The Levites are to build an altar, and erect plastered pillars on which the words of the Torah will be inscribed. The Levites shall then proclaim in a loud voice a series of curses that will befall the people if they do not uphold the covenant, and a series of blessings that will accrue to them if they fulfill the covenant.

Some readers may notice anomalies in this passage. Don't the Children of Israel already have tablets inscribed with the Torah? Why do they need plastered pillars? And what are they doing on the sacred mountains in Shechem? Will not Jerusalem be the eternal center of the covenant? These and other inconsistencies in the Torah have led scholars to theorize about the differing traditions of the northern and southern tribes of Israel—the northern tribes with their center and holy mountain in Shechem, and the southern tribes with their center and holy mountain in Jerusalem. These competing traditions were ultimately woven together in the final version of the Torah that we hold today.

That said, I wish to focus on the dramatic ritual itself. The 12 tribes are arrayed on opposite slopes, and the Levites proclaim 12 prohibitions, followed by a communal "Amen." The number 12 would appear to parallel the number of tribes, and continue the symmetry of the entire description, but as I read the passage, I asked myself, out of all the *mitzvot* in the Torah, why are these 12 placed together here? Listen to some of the prohibitions:

> Cursed be anyone who makes a graven image and sets it up in secret—and all the people shall respond, "Amen."
>
> Cursed be the one who insults father or mother—and all the people shall respond, "Amen."
>
> Cursed be the one who moves a neighbor's landmark—and all the people shall respond, "Amen."
>
> Cursed be the one who misdirects a blind person on the way—and all the people shall respond, "Amen."
>
> Cursed be the one who subverts the rights of the stranger, the orphan and the widow—and all the people shall respond, "Amen."

Then follow several prohibitions against incestuous relationships, followed by:

> Cursed be the one who strikes down a fellow in secret—and all the people shall respond, "Amen."
>
> Cursed be the one who accepts a bribe in the case of the murder of an innocent person—and all the people shall respond, "Amen."
>
> Cursed be whoever will not uphold the terms of this Teaching and observe them—and all the people shall respond, "Amen" (Deuteronomy 27:15–19, 24–26).

Upon my first reading, this collection of "Thou Shalt Not's" appeared random. But then I noticed a common thread: All of these transgressions can be performed in secret. Each one is something a person could get away with: hiding a graven image, murdering someone in a dark alley, taking money under the table, engaging in illicit sex, misdirecting a blind person, moving a landmark in the dark of night . . . who will ever know?

It appears that the Children of Israel are being directed here to affirm a higher level of moral responsibility. They are being asked to become people of conscience. One level of moral decision-making is based on what would happen to you if you got caught. You don't want to look bad. You don't want to be punished or shamed or ruin your reputation, so you avoid transgression. This external focus is important, especially when it reinforces upright behavior. But an ethically mature person has internalized that witness. That person no longer determines his or her behavior on whether someone else is watching because the ethically mature person is already and always watching him or herself, assessing the rightness of the action at hand.

I think that upon Mount Ebal and Mount Gerizim the Children of Israel are being recruited into a higher and more mature level of moral behavior. As they enter the Promised Land, they will no longer have Moses to guide them. They will no longer be traveling together in a self-contained camp. They will now be spread out over a large land, each tribe occupying its own territory. They need to build a trustworthy community. Each person must carry a witness within.

The reading of *Ki Tavo* always falls as the High Holy Days approach, and it is a timely teaching. During this season of repentance, we are each called upon to do a חֶשְׁבּוֹן נֶפֶשׁ *heshbon nefesh*, a rigorous self-accounting. We are asked to assess whether we have harmed anyone, and whether we need to make amends and offer apologies to others whose lives we have touched. Let's not separate our account sheet between overt and hidden transgressions. I believe that our Torah portion is reminding us that, for a person of conscience, there are no hidden transgressions. We need to do our utmost to be honest witnesses of our own behavior and to hold ourselves to a high standard. Amen to that!

51 ——————————————————————

Nitzavim | נצבים

Choose Life!

הַעִדֹתִי בָכֶם הַיּוֹם אֶת־הַשָּׁמַיִם וְאֶת־הָאָרֶץ הַחַיִּים וְהַמָּוֶת
נָתַתִּי לְפָנֶיךָ הַבְּרָכָה וְהַקְּלָלָה וּבָחַרְתָּ בַּחַיִּים לְמַעַן תִּחְיֶה
אַתָּה וְזַרְעֶךָ:

*Ha'idoti va'khem ha'yom et ha'shamayim v'et ha'aretz:
ha'khayim v'ha'mavet natati l'fanekha, ha'brakhah
v'ha'klalah. u'vakharta ba'khayim, l'ma'an tikhyeh
atah v'zarekha.*

I call heaven and earth to witness against you this day: I have
put before you life and death, blessing and curse. Choose
life, that you and your descendants may live! (Deuteronomy
30:19).

THIS WEEK'S TORAH PORTION, *Nitzavim*, is always read on the Shabbat
preceding Rosh Hashanah. I praise the wisdom of our sages, who carefully
calibrated the calendar so that these words would prime us for the New
Year. It is Moses's final oration (although a coda of an epic poem and a
blessing will follow) and ends with the stirring call that has come to define
the Jewish character, and especially this season of the Jewish year: Choose

life. Moses's words are so timeless that I feel he could be delivering them in our synagogues today.

Moses makes clear that he is speaking across the generations, addressing every single individual—from the leaders to the woodchoppers; men, women and children; and even those who are not yet present to hear him speak (Deuteronomy 29:9–14). He calls us to do תְּשׁוּבָה *teshuvah*, to return to God, to our people, to our land (Deuteronomy 30:1–5). He calls us to open our hearts, "to love the Source of Life with all of your heart and soul" (Deuteronomy 30:6). He insists that this change of heart is possible, and that we do not need intermediaries to accomplish it:

> Surely, this teaching which I enjoin upon you this day is not too baffling for you, nor is it beyond reach. It is not in the heavens, that you should say, "Who among us can go up to the heavens and get it for us and impart it to us, that we may do it?" Neither is it beyond the sea, that you should say, "Who among us can cross to the other side of the sea and get it for us and impart it to us, that we may do it?" No, the thing is very close to you, in your own mouth and in your own heart, that you may do it. See, I set before you this day life and goodness, and death and evil (Deuteronomy 30:11–15).

Moses asserts that we are capable of change. He insists that we are capable of opening our hearts, of choosing life and goodness, no matter how far we have strayed from our goal: "Even if you are scattered at the ends of the world, from there YHVH will gather you, and bring you back" (Deuteronomy 30:4).

Moses is being the ultimate spiritual teacher here at the end of his teaching. He is telling us that our self-limiting beliefs are keeping us from fully participating in the unfolding of creation. This *Torah,* this teaching, is not in heaven or across the sea. It is close to you, on your own lips and in your own heart. You can do it! I feel Moses's sense of urgency as he exhorts us, his people, to enter the Promised Land—the land of human fulfillment. Our noble task is to expand our sense of the possible. We are to do *teshuvah,* and align our beliefs about ourselves with our true and magnificent potential. We are to choose life and aliveness so that, as Moses says, we and our descendants may live long upon the good earth that the Creator has granted to us.

This is the message of the High Holy Days. This is the message of Judaism.

We aim to give up our acquired habit of powerlessness—the idea that we cannot change—and, trembling at times, crack open the door or the window again to new possibilities, and let the breeze rush into our closed room. We aim to open our hearts, even if that means opening ourselves to uncertainty and pain. We aim to come home—to ourselves, to our community, to life and aliveness, from wherever we have wandered or felt exiled.

I love that Moses calls heaven and earth as witnesses to this moment, as if to say, we are not separate from creation. The whole world is watching, as it were, waiting for us to fulfill our part. The life energy that animates all of creation also animates us. One day that energy will carry each of us out of our individuality, and our essence will rejoin and mingle with the earth and sky. That will be the day of our death. But now, Moses asks heaven and earth to witness us—each of us empowered to be a conduit for love, righteousness, courage and transformation. We matter. The Baal Shem Tov taught that Divine sparks are hidden and trapped throughout creation, waiting to be liberated, and that every single person has their own unique set of Divine sparks waiting for them to reveal and uplift. No one else can fulfill the noble task of being you. As Rabbi Abraham Joshua Heschel taught, "The challenge I face is how to actualize the quiet eminence of my being."

Yes, it is a challenging time. We can list the reasons to despair. Then again, when have times not been challenging? No matter, says Moses, the potential for change is still in our hands.

Speaking across the ages, Moses still has an audience for his words each time we begin another new year: "I have put before you life and death, blessing and curse. Choose life!"

52

Vayeilekh | וילך

Take Courage!

חִזְקוּ וְאִמְצוּ!

Hizku v'imtzu!

Be strong and courageous! (Deuteronomy 31:6).

VAYEILEKH HAS THE FEWEST verses of any Torah portion and takes up just one chapter: Chapter 31 of Deuteronomy. Except during Jewish leap years, *Vayeilekh* is paired with *Nitzavim*, and together they make up one of several "double portions" in the annual cycle of readings. Between the fact that *Nitzavim* overshadows *Vayeilekh* with some of the most famous rhetoric of the entire Torah—Moses's exhortation to us to "choose life!"—and the fact that *Vayeilekh* is always read just before or after Rosh Hashanah, *Vayeilekh* rarely gets much attention. But it merits a close reading.

Vayeilekh opens with Moses announcing to the Children of Israel that his death is imminent: "I am now 120 years old, and I am no longer able to be active. YHVH has told me 'You shall not go across yonder Jordan' " (Deuteronomy 31:2). Moses reminds them that it is now Joshua who will lead them into the Promised Land.

I have learned that, in any given passage, the Torah makes its theme clear through the repetition of key words and phrases. In the brief text of *Vayeilekh*, one phrase is heard in refrain: Be strong and courageous. First, from Moses to the Children of Israel:

> Be strong and courageous, be not in fear or dread of [your en-
> emies, as you take possession of the Promised Land] (Deuter-
> onomy 31:6).

Then from Moses to Joshua:

> Then Moses called Joshua and said to him in the sight of all Israel,
> "Be strong and courageous, for it is you who shall go with this
> people into the land that YHVH swore to their ancestors to give
> them . . . YHVH will be with you; YHVH will not fail you or for-
> sake you. Fear not, and be not dismayed!" (Deuteronomy 31:7–8).

And then, as if in crescendo, YHVH charges Joshua directly:

> Be strong and courageous, for you shall bring the Children of Is-
> rael into the land that I promised them on oath, and I will be with
> you (Deuteronomy 31:23).

In the literary structure of Deuteronomy, this theme at the end of Moses's oration evokes the book's very beginning. The book of Deuteronomy is Moses's recounting of all the events that have befallen the Children of Israel over the past 40 years of wandering. He is speaking to a new generation, born in the wilderness, which has not known slavery nor seen the miracles of liberation from slavery or the revelation at Mount Sinai. Knowing that he himself will soon be gone, Moses must impart the sacred history and purpose that have guided the Children of Israel thus far, so that they might carry it on after Moses passes away. Curiously, Moses does not begin by telling the story of the Exodus or Mount Sinai. Instead, he recounts the story of the 12 scouts who reconnoitered the Promised Land 39 years earlier. Upon their return, despite reporting positively on the bounty of the land they had explored, 10 of the scouts were terrified by the strength and size of the land's inhabitants, and upon hearing this, the Children of Israel's hearts melted away, and they demanded to return to Egypt. Moses says, "I then said to you, have no fear or dread of them for YHVH will go before you and fight on your behalf, just as took place in Egypt!" (Deuteronomy 1:29–30).

As you may recall, because of the scouts' failure of nerve and the Children of Israel's loss of courage, YHVH determines that they are not ready to enter the Promised Land, and instead decrees that they will wander for 40 years, until the generation from Egypt have all passed away. Then, perhaps, a new generation will be ready to take possession of their goal. Only Joshua and Caleb, the two scouts who tried to encourage the Children of Israel, will live to see that day.

As the Children of Israel stand on the far side of the Jordan, knowing that the only leader they have ever known will not be crossing over with them, this is the central message that Moses wants them to hear: You will never attain your goal without courage. Even at this most terrifying moment, when you must cross into the unknown on your own, you must not allow yourselves to be ruled by fear and dread, or your hearts will melt away. You will lose your resolve. This is what happened to your ancestors; they lost their resolve, and they lost their way. Moses opens his words with this message at the outset of Deuteronomy, and now he closes with it in *Vayeilekh*.

This is the Torah's message to us whenever we stand on the cusp of the next challenging endeavor: Be strong and courageous. Do not live in fear or dread. Know that YHVH, Life Unfolding, is always with you, supporting you and sustaining you on your journey through life. Our journeys are not necessarily epic, and our challenges may be private and visible only to a few. Nevertheless, every day we face these challenges—whether it is fighting through pain in a physical therapy session, or taking a principled position, or not giving up on our goals. But whether or not our challenges appear small or large to our own eyes, it's always up to us to act with courage and to take that next step across the River Jordan. That's the only way to get to the Promised Land.

53 ————————————————

Ha'azinu | האזינו

Holy Metaphors

וַיֵּנִקֵהוּ דְבַשׁ מִסֶּלַע וְשֶׁמֶן מֵחַלְמִישׁ צוּר:

Va'yeinikeihu d'vash misela, v'shemen mei'khalmish tzur.

God suckled them with honey from the rock, with rich oil from the flinty crag (Deuteronomy 32:13).

HA'AZINU ("GIVE EAR" OR "Listen") is one of two poems attributed to Moses. In Exodus 15, he leads the Children of Israel in שִׁירַת הַיָּם *Shirat Ha'yam*, the "Song of the Sea," after they have crossed the Sea of Reeds to safety. Now, at the very end of the journey, Moses imparts this epic poem.

The Hebrew of *Ha'azinu* is exalted, the language wonderfully rich. We are reminded that the Torah is a great literary creation. Ancient Hebrew poetry did not utilize rhyme, but is rich in assonance, rhythm, meter and repetition. It's beautiful. The poem opens:

> Give ear, O heavens, let me speak
> Let the earth hear the words I utter!
> May my discourse come down as the rain,
> My speech distill as the dew,

Like showers on young growth,

Like droplets on the grass.

Moses then paints verbal pictures of the long relationship of YHVH with the Children of Israel. Moses likens God to a father who watches over Israel, the apple of his eye. But God is equally likened to a nursing mother, and to an eagle hovering over her nestlings and bearing them gently on her pinions. God finds Israel as a foundling in the howling wilderness, and rescues her and raises her, but Israel becomes a spoiled child, grown fat and rebellious. In another section, God is likened to an avenging warrior with a flashing sword, routing Israel's enemies.

This plethora of metaphors makes clear that the Torah does not have a singular or literal description of YHVH, the Source of Life. How could that which is infinite be captured in a single image? I'm certain that one of the reasons that the Second Commandment forbids making an image of God is the fundamental truth that God transcends form and cannot be contained in any fixed image or phrase. The Torah abounds in descriptive names and adjectives for YHVH, and that poetic approach to speaking about God continues in Judaism to this day. A literal and reductive approach to Torah will always miss the point; one cannot speak about God in literal terms, and our ancestors understood this. They instead offered abounding metaphors.

This abundance of imagery frees us to choose the metaphors that resonate for us at any given moment of our lives. If we feel abandoned in a howling wilderness, perhaps we can imagine God as mother, grabbing us up and clutching us to her breast. If we are overcome by awe, perhaps God can be a Sovereign of the Heavenly Hosts, presiding in majesty over the cosmos. If we are facing a struggle, perhaps God can be the warrior, striding ahead of us and clearing the path. But God is not limited to anthropomorphism. Sometimes, God is a quality in the natural world: In some places in the Torah, we find God described as the Breath of All Life; in others, God is the Source of Living Waters. God is also named by abstract qualities: הָרַחֲמָן *Ha'rakhaman*—the Compassionate; even שָׁלוֹם *Shalom*—Peace. And all these names—infinite metaphors, in fact—are subsumed within God's ineffable name YHVH, a name we do not pronounce and which contains all multitudes. Perhaps awed silence is our most certain recourse for naming the unnamable. Yet language is also sublime, and so out of the silence, we offer God names.

In *Ha'azinu*, one metaphor appears eight times, far more than any other: God as צוּר *Tzur*, Rock. I find this metaphor compelling: God as our

Rock, צוּר יִשְׂרָאֵל *Tzur Yisrael*, "The Rock of Israel"; our foundation, solid and everlasting; our source of stability and support; a place to stand firm; an elevated place; a fortress; a refuge. As I let my imagination play over this metaphor, as I see myself stand on that rock, I feel more grounded, balanced and powerful.

Ha'azinu soars, moving into the transcendent. God is not merely a solid, unmoving rock. God is a rock that also flows with sustenance: "God suckled them with honey from the rock, with rich oil from the flinty crag" (Deuteronomy 32:13).

How rich, indeed! Imagine a rock that also produces nourishment. Honey and oil! YHVH, the Source of Life, is both stability and flow, security and sustenance. A nursing mother, maybe Mother Earth herself: A rock that sustains us!

God as the sustaining rock in the wilderness is a frequent metaphor in the *Tanach* (Hebrew Bible). Repeatedly, we hear the famous story of God instructing Moses to draw water from the rock so that the parched people can drink (e.g., Exodus 17:6, Deuteronomy 8:15, Isaiah 48:21, Psalms 78:20, Psalms 105:41). Psalm 114, from the *Hallel* psalm cycle, concludes that YHVH is the one "who turns the rock into a pool of water, the flint into a bubbling spring."

YHVH is the power in the universe—and also inside us—that can take a problem and find an unexpected solution. YHVH can take an apparently immovable object and find an opening through which to pass. YHVH can take a hardened heart and crack it open, so that tears and life pour forth. The world, and each of us, is filled with unseen life and possibility. This hidden potential can be made manifest by the skillful application of love and vision, patience, trust and faith. Even a rock can turn into a bubbling spring! Dr. Martin Luther King liked to say, "God is the power in the universe that can make a way out of no way." I might add: God is the power inherent in every human being that can let the sweet honey of life flow through even the most armored heart.

I might also add: May your encounters with Torah flow with sweet nourishment for your soul. May you be suckled with honey from the rock, with rich oil from the flinty crag. May my discourse come down as the rain, and my speech distill as dew: may holy metaphors animate your inner life.

54 ─────────────────────

Vezot Haberakhah | וזאת הברכה

Moses Teaches Us How to Die

וְזֹאת הַבְּרָכָה אֲשֶׁר בֵּרַךְ מֹשֶׁה אִישׁ הָאֱלֹהִים אֶת־בְּנֵי יִשְׂרָאֵל לִפְנֵי מוֹתוֹ:

Vezot haberakhah asher beirakh Moshe, ish haʾelohim, et Bʾnei Yisrael lifnei moto.

This is the blessing with which Moses, the man of God, bade the Children of Israel farewell before he died (Deuteronomy 33:1).

THAT POIGNANT LINE OPENS the very last portion of the entire Torah, *Vezot Haberakhah*—"This Is the Blessing." Oddly, this is the one and only Torah portion that is never read as part of the annual weekly cycle of reading. The only time it is heard in synagogue is on the holiday of *Simchat Torah*. Because *Vezot Haberakhah* is not part of the regular rhythm of Torah readings, we don't study this portion with regularity.

The *parashah* begins with a lengthy poem in which Moses gives a specific blessing to each of the tribes of Israel. Then in the final chapter of the Torah, we hear about Moses's death: "Moses ascended from the plains of Moab to the summit of Mount Nebo, across from Jericho, and YHVH showed him the entire land . . ." (Deuteronomy 34:1).

Moses looks out over the entire Promised Land, which he will never enter, and he dies on the mountaintop. The people mourn, and the Torah ends, "Never again did there arise a prophet like Moses, who knew YHVH face to face . . . and displayed YHVH's great and awesome might before all of Israel" (Deuteronomy 34:10, 12).

In its typically succinct way, the Torah does not elaborate greatly on Moses's death. He goes up to the mountaintop, views the Promised Land from afar and dies. But in an anonymous, seventh-century *midrash* collection called פְּטִירַת מֹשֶׁה *Petirat Moshe*—"The Death of Moses"—a fully human Moses emerges, ambivalent and conflicted, to confront his own death. In classic *midrashic* fashion, *Petirat Moshe* draws out clues in the Torah text to tell a much more nuanced and elaborate story. In the *midrashic* retelling, Moses becomes an everyman, an everywoman, and we see ourselves reflected in the text.[1] The *midrash* tells us:

> Moses waited forty years before approaching God with his request to be permitted to enter the Promised Land with the Children of Israel. When God commanded him to appoint Joshua as his successor, Moses finally saw that God actually intended for him to die without entering the Promised Land, although God had decreed so ten times. Moses had thought: "Look how often God annulled the punishments he had decreed for the people, whenever I intervened on their behalf! Surely God will accept my prayers on my own behalf."

The first reaction of Moses to the awareness that he is soon to die is to ignore it. So it is with all of us. I will walk away from a dying person's hospital bedside, full of the consciousness of death and the poignant preciousness of life, and literally within minutes, I'll be composing my "to do" list for the rest of the day. We are, all of us, so deeply attached to life.

The *midrash* continues: But on the seventh day of Adar, Moses hears a heavenly voice, "Take heed, O Moses, for you have only one more day to live." What does he do then? As Louis Ginsberg writes it, "He wrote thirteen

---

1. My source is Louis Ginzberg's *Legends of the Jews*, an indispensable resource for the investigation of Jewish lore.

scrolls of the Torah, thinking, 'If I occupy myself with the Torah, which is the tree of life, this day will draw to a close, and the impending doom will be as naught.'"

Moses tries to outwit death, to outflank the מַלְאַךְ הַמָּוֶת *Malakh Hamavet*—the "Angel of Death." Welcoming our death is only the last resort. We busy ourselves, fill our moments with the details of living, distract ourselves from the void that hovers at the edge of our every day. Yet Moses does realize that his activity, no matter how righteous, cannot stave off the decree, and so he begins to bargain. Joshua and all of Israel are sitting before him when a voice from heaven again breaks through: "Moses, you now have only four hours of life." The *midrash* continues:

Now Moses began to implore God anew: "רִבּוֹנוֹ שֶׁל עוֹלָם *Ribono shel olam*![2] If I must die only for my disciple Joshua's sake, consider that I am willing to conduct myself as if I were his pupil; let it be as if he were high priest, and I a common priest; he a king, and I his servant." God replied: "I have sworn by My great Name, which 'the heaven and heaven of heavens cannot contain,' that you shall not cross the Jordan." Moses: "*Ribono shel olam*, let me at least, by the power of the ineffable Name, fly like a bird in the air; or make me like a fish, transform my two arms to fins and my hair to scales, that like a fish I may leap over the Jordan and see the land of Israel." God: "No one can avert the decree." Moses: "*Ribono shel olam*, cut me up, limb by limb, throw me over the Jordan, and then revive me, so that I may see the land." God: "Moses, it is your time to die." Moses: "Let me at least skim the land with my glance." God: "In this point will I comply with thy wish."

Moses embodies our very human tendency to say "not yet!" God, just let me live until my grandson's bar mitzvah . . . until I finish writing that book . . . until my daughter finishes high school . . . until I can reach my goal . . . until I can see the Promised Land.

After Moses finishes looking upon the land, he is one hour nearer to death. A voice again sounds from heaven, warning him that there is no escape: He has three hours left. Moses keeps praying, however: *Ribono shel olam*, let me stay on this side of the Jordan. *Ribono shel olam*, even if I can't enter the Promised Land, let me live. Even as a beast of the field, let me live and see the world! Then God commands him to be silent.

---

2. רִבּוֹנוֹ שֶׁל עוֹלָם *Ribono Shel Olam* means "Master of the Universe," and is meant as a direct and intimate address to God.

Oh, this poignant desire: I just want to live! No goals, accomplishments, roles—just precious life itself! Once, when I was looking at the brilliance of the autumn leaves I said aloud, "Dear God, I couldn't bear to miss this sight; let me live."

Then the Children of Israel come to Moses to bid him farewell, but he says, "Wait . . . ."

This reminds me of bedtime when my kids were small. We are programmed to want to be awake and alive! We are voracious for life.

The *midrash* has thus far described all the strategies we humans have to focus on life in the face of death: denial, distraction, bargaining. But what is left to do when, as God says to Moses, "You have used too many words," and there is no recourse left but to acknowledge that our time on this earth will end?

This is the consciousness that Yom Kippur especially is intended to call forth. It is a day to confront our mortality head on. All the regular patterns of life are suspended. All the comfortable patterns are interrupted so that we might ask ourselves the terrifying yet vital question: In the full consciousness of my own mortality, how do I want to live? Traditionally, as Yom Kippur approaches, we visit our ancestors' graves in preparation. On the day itself, we purposefully remember the dead at *Yizkor*. We don't eat; we wear white. We approach death, rather than waiting for death to approach us. This is not morbid fascination, but part of the genius of Judaism that forces us to suspend all the strategies we normally employ to keep death at arm's length.

So, what does Moses now do? According to the *midrash*:

> The people now came to Moses and said, "The hour of your death is at hand," and he replied: "Wait—until I have blessed Israel. All my life long they had no pleasant experiences with me, for I constantly rebuked them and admonished them to fear God and fulfill the commandments, therefore do I not now wish to depart out of this world before I have blessed them."

Moses blesses the people and asks them to forgive his sternness. They do so, and in turn, they ask his forgiveness: "We have often kindled your anger and have laid many burdens upon you but forgive us now." Moses does so. He gathers the Children of Israel around him, he offers them his blessings, and he asks for their forgiveness as well. This is *teshuvah*. Before departing this life, Moses does his best to reconcile with his loved ones and with his extended family.

Now Moses is ready. People come to him and say, "The time has come." Moses says, "Blessed be God." Yet even then, our tradition portrays Moses as nothing more than human:

Moses said, "I pray you, when you shall have entered into the land of Israel, remember me still, and my bones, and say, 'Woe to Moses who ran before us like a horse, but whose bones remained in the desert.'"

Fully accepting his fate, Moses nevertheless has regrets about his unmet life's goal, the Promised Land. We are complicated like Moses—accepting death yet still, ever, ever desiring life. We are human.

Then the people say to Moses, "What will become of us when you are gone?" He tells them to place their trust in God and urges them to dwell in peace, and promises to see them again in the "world to come." Then everybody weeps, with lamentations that reach to the heavens.

We weep, for the love we shared and for the love we have never succeeded in sharing. We weep, for the utter joy of being here and the sorrow knowing that we will one day have to leave. Our hearts break and overflow with tears. On a beautiful radio program, the host explained that when she was a child, she didn't understand why the adults cried on Yom Kippur. She hadn't lived long enough. But now she cries with them.

Finally, Moses lays down on his deathbed. He is ready. The Torah states that Moses then died עַל־פִּי יהוה *al pi Adonai*, usually translated as "at the command of God." But the Hebrew can also mean, Moses died "from the mouth of God." And so, the *midrash* explains: God took Moses's soul by kissing him on the mouth. Moses dies with a kiss from God.

And here, we reach the very end of the Torah. God draws the breath of life from Moses, and that breath returns to the Source. But this portion never stands alone in the Jewish liturgical cycle. When the death of Moses is chanted on *Simchat Torah*, it is immediately followed by the chanting of Genesis, In the Beginning: "And YHVH blew the breath of life into the human's nostrils, and the human became a living being" (Genesis 2:7). Perhaps our sages wanted us to read the very end of the Torah only in conjunction with the very beginning. Perhaps our sages wanted to remind us that although the Breath of Life will be withdrawn from each of us when our time comes, other beings will receive that Breath in their turn, and Life will always return and be restored in new form. Perhaps our sages placed this confluence on the festival of *Simchat Torah*, the festival of rejoicing and dancing with the Torah, so that we can practice rejoicing with our entire beings, aware that our length of days here is unknown, knowing that our life has been breathed into us. And that one day, our time will come to offer it back, like a kiss, to the One who breathed life into us. While we are here, between that first and last breath, let us rejoice in the gift of life as fully as we are able.

CPSIA information can be obtained
at www.ICGtesting.com
Printed in the USA
BVHW080735201220
595725BV00008B/16

9 781725 251076